The Art of Functional Programming

with examples in OCaml, Haskell, and Java

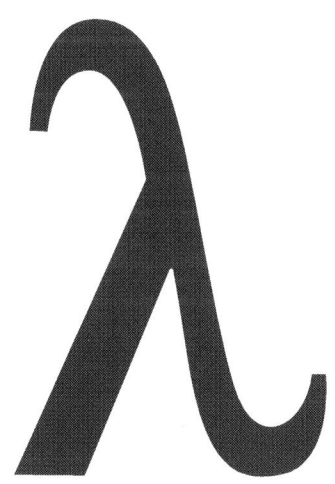

Minh Quang Tran, PhD

The Art of Functional Programming

Copyright © 2022 Minh Quang Tran.
All rights reserved.

About the author:

Minh Quang Tran has more than 20 years of experience studying software development and working in the software industry. He has worked in various tech startups and big software companies in Europe. He received his M.Sc. in Computer Science from McMaster University, Canada, and his Ph.D. in Computer Science from Technical University of Berlin, Germany. His interest lies in understanding and mastering the fundamentals and principles that cut across programming languages, frameworks, and tools.

Contents

1 Introduction   **4**
- 1.1 About This Book 4
- 1.2 A Bite of Functional Programming 8
- 1.3 Why Functional Programming Matters? 15
- 1.4 Required Tools 19
- 1.5 Quiz on Imperative vs. Functional Programming . . 23
- 1.6 Answers to Quiz on Imperative vs. Functional Programming 25

2 Expressions – Building Blocks of Functional Programs   **27**
- 2.1 Functional Programming is All About Expressions . 27
- 2.2 Syntax of Expressions 34
- 2.3 Parsing Expressions 41
- 2.4 Types of Expressions 49
- 2.5 Values of Expressions 57
- 2.6 Assign Names to Expressions 61
- 2.7 Programming Challenges 68
- 2.8 Solutions to Programming Challenges 70
- 2.9 Quiz on Expressions 70
- 2.10 Answers to Quiz on Expressions 74

3 Building Abstractions with Functions   **77**
- 3.1 Lambda Calculus: Foundation of Functional Programming 77
- 3.2 Function Abstraction and Function Application . . . 84
- 3.3 Use Currying for Function Chaining 94

Contents

    3.4   Recursive Functions 99
    3.5   General Computation Methods as Higher-Order Functions 107
    3.6   Programming Challenges 116
    3.7   Solutions to Programming Challenges 120
    3.8   Quiz on Functions 122
    3.9   Answers to Quiz on Functions 127

4 Compound Data Types 130
    4.1   Group Data Objects into Tuples 130
    4.2   Destruct tuples with pattern matching 132
    4.3   Store Sequences of Data with Lists 136
    4.4   Declare User-defined Types with Algebraic Data Types 145
    4.5   Programming Challenges 158
    4.6   Solutions to Programming Challenges 161
    4.7   Quiz on Compound Datatypes 163
    4.8   Answers to Quiz on Compound Datatypes 170

5 Common Computation Patterns 173
    5.1   The map Function 173
    5.2   The filter function 187
    5.3   The fold function 191
    5.4   The zip Function 202
    5.5   Programming Challenges 206
    5.6   Solutions to Programming Challenges 210
    5.7   Quiz on Common Computation Patterns 212
    5.8   Answers to Quiz on Common Computation Patterns 217

Contents

6 Dataflow Programming with Functions   **220**
- 6.1   List-based Dataflow Programming 220
- 6.2   Stream-based Dataflow Programming 233
- 6.3   Programming Challenges 248
- 6.4   Solutions to Programming Challenges 250
- 6.5   Quiz on Dataflow Programming with Functions . . . 251
- 6.6   Answers to Quiz on Dataflow Programming with Functions 255

7 Applying Functional Programming in Practice   **258**
- 7.1   Handle Collections in Data Processing Applications   258
- 7.2   Handle JSON 267

8 Conclusion   **280**
- 8.1   Wrap Up 280
- 8.2   Where to Go from Here? 281

1 Introduction

1.1 About This Book

1.1.1 Book description

Welcome to *The Art of Functional Programming* book!

Functional programming is a powerful and elegant programming paradigm. Initially only popular among university researchers, it's gained much traction in the software industry in the last few years. From big companies to start-ups, engineers and managers have realized that functional programming excels at abstraction and composition. Functional programming allows for highly concise solutions with increased safety. This has led to rising demand for software engineers with functional programming skills. This book will help you move your programming skills to the next level.

This book is grounded on my beliefs about software development resulting from my reflection after many years of studying and working in the software industry. First, there are tons of programming languages, frameworks, and tools out there – with many more coming in the future. The only way to stay ahead of the game in this vast and quickly changing software industry is to master the fundamentals and principles that cut across programming languages, frameworks, and tools. In the case of functional programming, learning to adopt the functional way of solving problems is much more productive than memorizing how to write functional code in a particular language. This book teaches this functional way of thinking.

1 INTRODUCTION

We'll also learn many fundamental techniques from programming languages, such as parsing, compilation, and type checking.

Second, I believe that a technique or tool is not very useful if it does not help us solve real-world problems and make our lives easier. In this book, we'll only look at examples and exercises that are typically encountered in a programmer's day-to-day job. Furthermore, an entire chapter is dedicated to applying what we've learned to real-world scenarios. In particular, we'll use functional programming to process collections of data for an e-commerce application and handle the JSON datatype.

I like to think of the duality of striving to grasp the fundamental principles of the functional paradigm while applying it to real-world problems pragmatically as the yin and yang of the journey to master functional programming.

Figure 1: Yin and yang as a symbol of duality

Here is the summary of the chapters in this book:

- In Chapter 1: Introduction, we'll start the book with an introduction to functional programming. In particular, we'll see how it can overcome some of the inherent weaknesses of the

1 INTRODUCTION

imperative programming paradigm. We'll also discuss why functional programming matters to any software engineer.

- In Chapter 2: Expressions – The Building Blocks of Functional Programs, we examine expressions and how to build complex expressions from simpler ones. Three aspects of expressions – syntax, types, and semantics—will be covered. Along the way, we'll gain a much deeper understanding of how programming languages work, including parsing, type checking, interpretation, and compilation.

- In Chapter 3: Building Abstractions with Functions, we'll get to know lambda calculus – a mathematical model serving as the foundation of all functional programming languages. We'll learn how to capture computation patterns as functions. Finally, we'll discuss various techniques for working with functions such as currying, recursion, and higher-order functions.

- In Chapter 4: Complex Data Types, we'll focus on the complex data types typically found in functional programming languages, such as tuples and lists. Furthermore, we'll use algebraic data types to represent hierarchical data, and pattern matching to extract data from complex data types.

- In Chapter 5: Common Computation Patterns, we'll dive into some of the most common computation patterns, such as map, filter, fold, and zip. These functions capture highly general computation patterns on lists and other data structures that can be reused to formulate many other functions.

1 INTRODUCTION

- In Chapter 6: Dataflow Programming with Functions, we'll go over dataflow programming, a programming paradigm that emphasizes composing programs from existing components. We'll learn how functional programming allows us to do dataflow programming elegantly and reap all its benefits.

- In Chapter 7: Applying Functional Programming to Various Domains, we'll apply what we've learned to process collections of data commonly found in mobile and web applications, as well as backend services. Furthermore, we'll use functional programming to represent and handle JSON.

We'll mainly use OCaml and occasionally Haskel to demonstrate the key concepts and techniques of functional programming throughout the book. To contrast functional programming concepts with imperative ones, we'll use Java. Yet, it is essential to repeat that most functional programming techniques introduced in this book are universal. That means we can apply them to almost any programming language that supports the functional programming style. This includes but is not limited to Swift, Kotlin, JavaScript, Go, Python, and even Java (using the Java Stream API).

1.1.2 Intended audience

This is a beginner and intermediate book aimed at software engineers, engineering managers, or computer science students interested in understanding the essence of functional programming. It is also an excellent fit for individuals who are currently preparing

1 INTRODUCTION

for coding interviews and want to improve their problem-solving skills.

1.2 A Bite of Functional Programming

Functional programming is a **programming paradigm** — a style or a way of thinking when writing software programs. There are many programming paradigms available, some of which are presented in the following diagram.

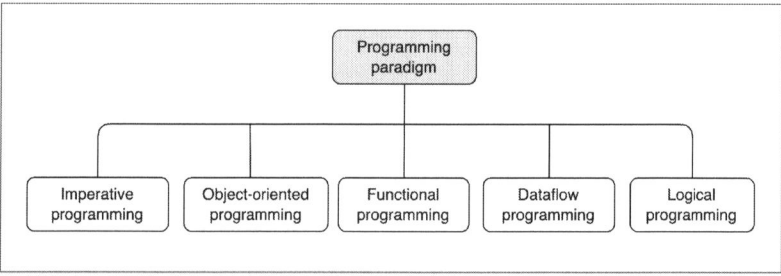

Figure 2: Programming paradigms

The **imperative programming paradigm** is the oldest, and still the most popular, paradigm used today. As the term "imperative" indicates, this paradigm models a program as a sequence of commands that change a program's state – "first do this, then do that." Even if we follow the object-oriented programming paradigm by encapsulating logic into classes, we'll likely implement the class methods in the imperative style.

Why has imperative programming dominated the programming world? In his Turing Award lecture titled *Can Programming Be*

1 INTRODUCTION

Liberated from the von Neumann Style? A Functional Style and Its Algebra of Programs, the computer scientist John Backus gives an insightful answer. According to his observation, the reason can be traced back to the **Von Neumann architecture**. Named after the mathematician John von Neumann, who took inspiration from the Turing machine, it is a computer architecture used by most computers produced today.

In the following, we'll review the von Neumann architecture and discuss several problems of the imperative programming paradigm due to its tight coupling with this architecture. Then we'll see how the functional programming paradigm can elegantly overcome those problems.

1.2.1 Von Neumann architecture

In its simplest form, a Von Neumann computer consists of a Central Processing Unit (CPU), a memory, and a bus that connects them. The CPU acts as the brain of the computer with the ability to execute a predefined set of machine code instructions. These instructions are in binary form, consisting of 0s and 1s, and do a very primitive thing, such as adding two numbers or testing whether a number equals zero or not. The CPU has a handful of registers to store data needed when executing an instruction.

The memory is the place where a program and its data are stored. A program is a sequence of machine code instructions. The CPU and the memory are connected via a bus. Due to this, a subset of machine code instructions is dedicated to loading data from mem-

1 INTRODUCTION

ory onto the registers or storing the data from the register onto the memory.

The following diagram illustrates the Von Neumann architecture.

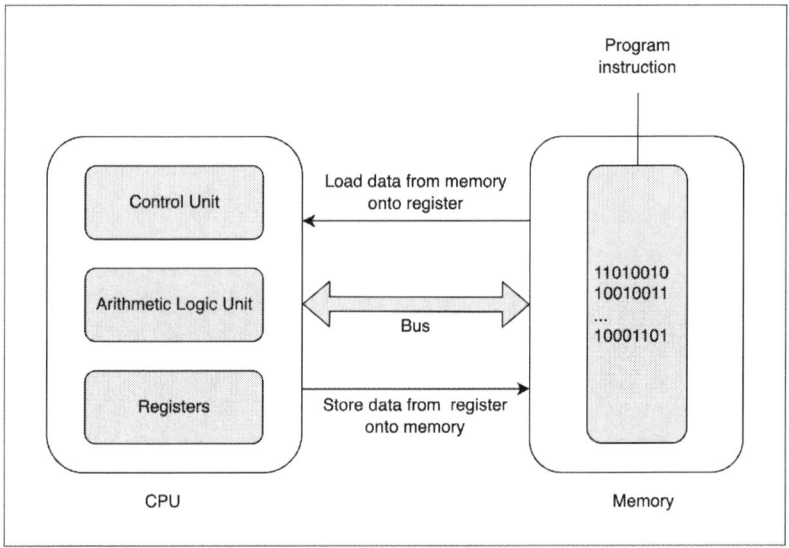

Figure 3: The von Neumann architecture

So, how does a program run? It's quite simple. The CPU runs the program following a mechanical **fetch-execute cycle**. First, it fetches the first instruction in the program and executes it. Then it fetches the next instruction and executes it, and this cycle continues on. Some instructions affect the order of execution. For instance, a jump instruction directs the CPU to jump back to a previous point of the instruction sequence. A branch instruction tells the CPU to branch to a particular instruction if some condition is true, for

1 INTRODUCTION

example, if two registers have the same values. These instructions are typically combined to implement loops and if-statements.

1.2.2 Low-level nature of imperative programming

Let's stop for a moment and reflect on the thought process when programming for the Von Neumann computer. A program is constructed as a sequence of instructions whose main task is to move data back and forth between the CPU and memory. These instructions also perform arithmetic and logical operations. The primary concern is how to update the memory cells in a stepwise manner. This model of programming for the Von Neumann architecture is the essence of what imperative programming is about.

Consider, for instance, an example of calculating the sum of squares of the first n numbers in the imperative style.

```
int sum = 0; i = 0;
while (i < n) {
    i = i + 1;
    sum = sum + i * i;
}
```

This program might be written with a high-level language, such as C, Java, or Python. Yet, the code is nothing more than a sequence of statements telling the physical computer how to update the memory. In particular, the variables sum and i correspond to the memory cells. An assignment statement, such as i = i + 1, equals moving the data from the memory to the CPU's registers, asking the CPU to perform the addition, and moving the data from the regis-

1 INTRODUCTION

ters to the memory to update the memory cell occupied by `i`. The `while` loop corresponds to how a physical computer uses branch and jump instructions to execute instructions repeatedly so long as the condition is still valid.

Its coupling with the Von Neumann architecture makes the imperative programming paradigm quite limited when it comes to forming abstractions and compositions when constructing programs.

1.2.3 Functional programming can do better

Let's use the functional programming paradigm to calculate the sum of squares of the first n numbers and compare the functional version with the imperative one.

Imperative style

```
1  int sum = 0; i = 0;
2  while (i <= n) {
3      i = i + 1;
4      sum = sum + i * i;
5  }
```

Functional style

```
1  (fold (+) 0 . map square) [1..n]
```

The imperative program is just a sequence of low-level statements for updating variables rather than constructed from simpler parts. The loop is a single unit and cannot be broken into smaller components. In contrast, the functional program is built from reusable parts. Only the functions – `square`, addition (`+`), and the initial

1 INTRODUCTION

value 0 – are specific to this program. The rest is assembled from general-purpose components, such as `map`, `fold`, and function composition. In particular, `map` applies a given function to all list elements, whereas `fold` combines elements in a list using a function, starting from an initial value. The function composition operator, `.`, allows us to turn the output of one function into the input of another one.

In fact, we can view the functional program above as a dataflow program that emphasizes the composability of this solution.

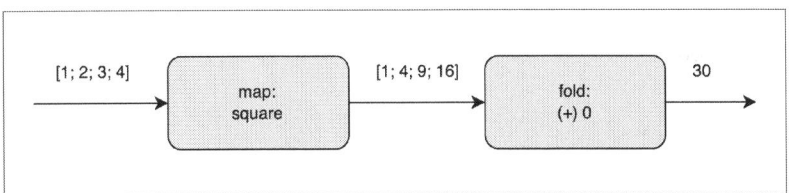

Figure 4: Functional program viewed as dataflow program

Another critical difference is that the first program is imperative, while the second one is descriptive. More specifically, the imperative program contains a sequence of commands stating how to initialize variables and update them in each step. The downside is we must mentally execute it to understand what it does, which requires a higher cognitive load. The functional program is declarative because it describes what the program does rather than how each step is computed. We can grasp the program based on its structure in one fell swoop without mentally executing it.

Now assume we would like to write another program that computes

The Art of Functional Programming

1 INTRODUCTION

the sum of squares of only prime numbers between 1 and n. Using the imperative style, we can copy the code of the old program and add an `if` statement.

```
int sum = 0; i = 0;
while (i <= n) {
    i = i + 1;
    if (isPrime(i)) {
        sum = sum + i * i;
    }
}
```

Here, we assume `isPrime` is a method that returns **true** if the argument is a prime and returns **false** otherwise.

However, in the functional programming paradigm, the solution is much more elegant.

```
(fold (+) 0 . map square . filter isPrime)
    [1..n];;
```

Compared to the imperative version, this program has a higher degree of **composability**, with functions readily combined into more powerful constructs. Here, we plug in another general-purpose function called `filter` to choose prime numbers from the list before passing them to `map` and then `fold`.

Let's look at the data flow diagram below:

1 INTRODUCTION

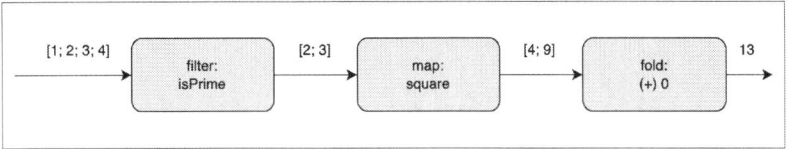

Figure 5: Calculate sum of squares of prime numbers in functional style

It is important to emphasize that it's by no means the purpose of this comparison to show that functional programming is *better* than imperative programming. As with any tool, way of thinking, or method of solving problems, each programming paradigm is more suitable for particular situations and less for others. Developing an intuition to decide when to use what tool and method is part of becoming an expert in any field, including programming. This book aims to help us develop this intuition so that we'll know when to utilize the power of functional programming and when not to.

1.3 Why Functional Programming Matters?

Are you a professional software engineer or aspire to become one? If yes, functional programming is undoubtedly among the most valuable skills to learn. This section will show why every software engineer should learn functional programming and why the best time to start is today.

1 INTRODUCTION

1.3.1 Powerful problem-solving tool

Learning functional programming means you acquire a new tool to solve problems. As with any craftsmanship, the more tools you have mastered and have at your disposal, the more skillful you become. In his insightful essay *Teach Yourself Programming in Ten Years*, Peter Norvig recommends aspiring software engineers to "learn at least a half dozen programming languages. Include … one [language] that emphasizes functional abstraction (like Lisp or ML or Haskell)". Both programming languages used in this book, OCaml and Haskell, are ML languages that emphasize functional abstraction.

Functional programming is a great tool to master because it can elegantly solve many programming problems in various domains. For instance, functional programming excels at applications that deal with hierarchical structures such as JSON and XML. Functional programming is also well suited to data processing in mobile apps, web apps, or backend services, especially when filtering, transforming, and aggregating data.

Even if we don't use functional programming in our day-to-day work, we still hugely benefit from learning it. Functional programming focuses on composition, or building complex programs from simpler ones, as well as on abstraction, or defining highly reusable general functions capturing common computation patterns. These are vital techniques for managing complexity when structuring code and building large software systems. As a result, learning the functional programming paradigm sharpens our ability to design software and write clean reusable code.

1   INTRODUCTION

1.3.2 The trend towards the declarative paradigm

The software industry has witnessed a gradual shift towards functional programming in recent years. Non-functional mainstream programming languages, such as Java, keep introducing features to write functional code. New programming languages, such as Elm, Elixir, Scala, Swift, and Kotlin, support functional programming from the ground up. Furthermore, more and more frameworks and libraries are heavily based on the functional programming paradigm, such as ReactiveX and Akka Streams. This implies that there is an increasing demand for software engineers with functional programming skills.

Interestingly, the trend towards functional programming is just a part of an overall transition from the imperative to the declarative paradigm in the software industry. Some of them are declarative UI, declarative build systems, declarative build pipelines, and even declarative deployment infrastructure.

1 INTRODUCTION

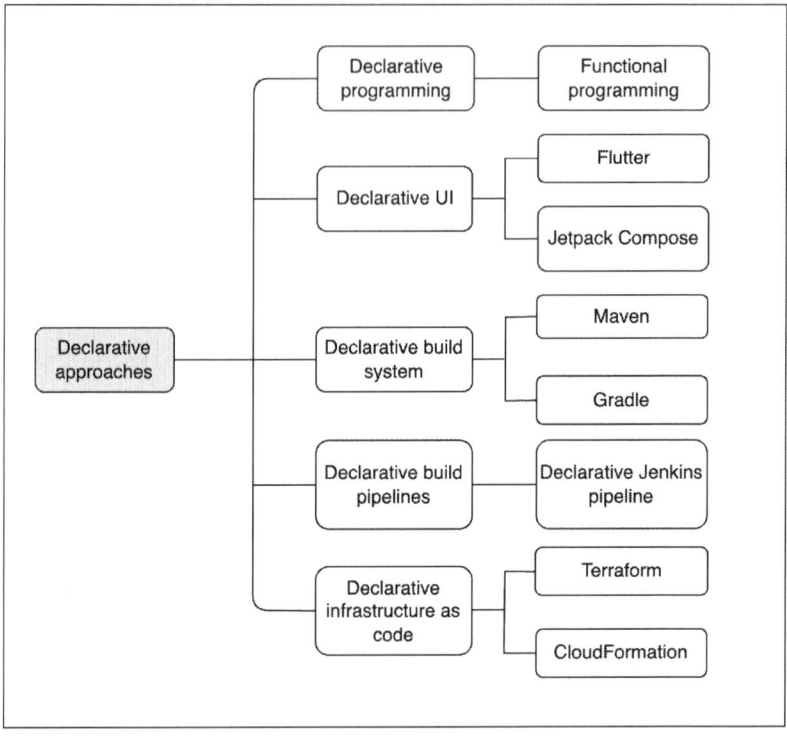

Figure 6: Use cases for declarative paradigm in software industry

Take build systems, for instance. The two most popular build systems today, Maven and Gradle, follow the declarative approach. We tell the system what we want to achieve, and the build system will figure out how to actually do it. This contrasts with imperative build systems like Ant, where we explicitly specify how the system should perform the build by listing an ordered sequence of the statements or commands.

Declarative build systems have many advantages compared to im-

1 INTRODUCTION

perative ones. In particular, they allow us to define a build system on a high level without caring about the implementation details. Moreover, they make it easier to create a complex build system from smaller build steps. The same can be said about declarative approaches for UI and infrastructure as code and so on.

Learning functional programming is an excellent way to adopt declarative thinking. It helps us see through many programming languages, frameworks, libraries, and build and deployment tools used in the software industry.

1.3.3 A new way of thinking

If you've never done functional programming before, some of the concepts and techniques in this book might feel awkward at first. This is totally normal, even expected. After all, you are acquiring a new way of thinking! As the computer scientist Alan Perlis puts it, "A language that doesn't affect the way you think about programming is not worth knowing." Regardless of your current level, this book is guaranteed to affect how you think about programming and make you a better software engineer.

1.4 Required Tools

This book contains many code examples in OCaml and Haskell to demonstrate functional programming. The fastest way is to simply enter those examples directly in a web browser using the two

1 INTRODUCTION

online tools *Try OCaml* (https://try.ocamlpro.com/) and *Try Haskell* (https://tryhaskell.org/).

If you want to try out these examples on your local machine, you must install OCaml and Haskell compilers. The following explains how to do so.

1.4.1 OCaml compiler

The recommended way to install the OCaml compiler on a local machine is to use the package manager OPAM. The instruction to do that can be found in this link https://opam.ocaml.org/doc/Install.html.

First, let's use the following script to install OPAM:

```
1  $ sh <(curl -sL https://raw.githubusercontent.
      com/ocaml/opam/master/shell/install.sh)
```

The script checks the architecture of the computer and downloads. It installs the suitable pre-compiled binary to `/usr/local/bin` by default.

Verify that OPAM has been installed successfully by typing in the terminal:

```
1  $ which opam
2  /usr/local/bin/opam
```

Next, use OPAM to install the latest OCaml compiler version. At the time of this writing, the newest OCaml compiler version is 4.12.0.

```
1  $ opam init
2  $ eval `opam env`
```

1 INTRODUCTION

```
3  $ opam switch create 4.12.0
4  $ eval `opam env`
```

The following tools have been installed:

- `ocamlc`: The OCaml bytecode compiler that compiles OCaml source files to bytecode files.
- `ocamlopt`: The OCaml native compiler that compiles OCaml source files to native code object files and links them to produce standalone executables.
- `ocamlrun`: The bytecode interpreter that executes bytecode files produced by `ocamlc`.

Verify that the OCaml bytecode compiler has been installed successfully before continuing.

```
1  $ which ocamlc
2  /Users/quang/.opam/4.12.0/bin/ocamlc
```

1.4.2 REPL utop

A great way to learn functional programming with OCaml on a local machine is using the read-eval-print loop (REPL) `utop`. Use the package manager `OPAM` mentioned previously to install `utop`.

```
1  $ opam install utop
```

You can start `utop` by entering it in the shell.

```
1  $ utop
```

1 INTRODUCTION

In utop, when you enter an expression that ends with ;; and press enter, utop displays the evaluated value.

```
1  utop # 1 + 2;;
2  - : int = 3
```

You can exit utop by the #quit command:

```
1  utop # #quit;;
```

Generally, it is a convention in utop that every expression ends with ;;. The following features are very useful while working in utop:

- We can press the "tab" key to auto-complete.
- We can press the "up" arrow key to browse the history of previously entered expressions.
- We can enter an expression in multiple lines as long as we haven't ended it with ;;

You can use utop to follow all OCaml code snippets listed in this book.

1.4.3 Haskell compiler

The most popular Haskell compiler is GHC (Glasgow Haskell Compiler). The official Haskell website contains installation instructions for GHC on all major platforms, including macOS, Linux, and Windows.

After the installation, verify that ghc is available.

```
1  $ which ghc
```

The Art of Functional Programming

1 INTRODUCTION

```
2  /Users/quang/.ghcup/bin/ghc
```

For this book, you can use the `ghci` REPL to write Haskell code and evaluate it directly.

```
1  $ which ghci
2  /Users/quang/.ghcup/bin/ghci
```

Run `ghci` and enter some Haskell expressions.

```
1  Prelude> 1 + 2 * 3
2  7
```

To exit `ghci`, use the `:quit` command.

1.5 Quiz on Imperative vs. Functional Programming

Let's test your understanding of why functional programming matters.

1.5.1 Quiz 1

Why is the ability to form abstraction and composition limited in the imperative programming paradigm?

Please select all following choices that apply.

Choice A: Because the imperative paradigm is conceptually tied to the Von Neumann computer architecture.

Choice B: Because imperative programming does not support functions.

1 INTRODUCTION

Choice C: Because imperative programming lacks combination operators.

1.5.2 Quiz 2

Which types of programming are programming paradigms?

Please select all following choices that apply.

Choice A: Imperative programming

Choice B: Functional programming

Choice C: Microservice

1.5.3 Quiz 3

Which classes of problems are suitable to be solved by the functional programming paradigm?

Please select all following choices that apply.

Choice A: Problems related to domain-specific languages (DSLs) and structures with a well-defined syntax such as JSON, XML, and so on.

Choice B: Problems involved lots of side-effects and mutating states

Choice C: Problems related to filtering, transforming, and aggregating collections of data.

1 INTRODUCTION

1.5.4 Quiz 4

Which tools and techniques follow the declarative approaches?

Please select all following choices that apply.

Choice A: Build tool Ant

Choice B: Build tool Maven

Choice C: Infrastructure as code software tool – Terraform

1.6 Answers to Quiz on Imperative vs. Functional Programming

1.6.1 Quiz 1

Choice A is correct. The imperative paradigm is based on how a physical computer works: moving data back and forth between the memory and CPU, updating memory cells. Due to this, abstraction and composition are limited in the imperative paradigm. The functional programming paradigm does not suffer from this limitation.

1.6.2 Quiz 2

Choice A and B are correct.

1.6.3 Quiz 3

Choice A is correct.

1.6.4 Quiz 4

Choice B and C are correct.

2 Expressions – Building Blocks of Functional Programs

2.1 Functional Programming is All About Expressions

Functional programming is all about evaluating expressions to values. For someone new to functional programming, this concept can be hard to grasp at first. A great way to understand it is by contrasting it with imperative programming.

In his Turing Award lecture *Can Programming Be Liberated from the von Neumann Style? A Functional Style and Its Algebra of Programs*, John Backus shows that an imperative programming language – such as C and Java – splits language elements into two worlds, expressions and statements. Expressions are those constructs that evaluate to values. In C or Java, we can define arithmetic expressions like `1 + 2`, boolean expressions like `true || false`, and string expressions like `"Hello"`. They all evaluate to values. Statements, on the other hand, are commands that perform something like variable assignment `s = s + 1`, `if` statements for branching, and `for/while` loops for executing statements repeatedly. Statements are characterized by their side effects.

Functional programming paradigm does not have any statements, no variable assignments, no `if` statements, and no `for/while` loops. Therefore, instead of variable assignments, we pass values around via function arguments and return values. Conditionals like `if` are expressions rather than statements. To formulate repeated computations, functional programming relies on recursive func-

2 EXPRESSIONS – BUILDING BLOCKS OF FUNCTIONAL PROGRAMS

tions instead of loops. Everything is an expression in the functional paradigm.

The following diagram compares the worldview difference between imperative and functional programming languages.

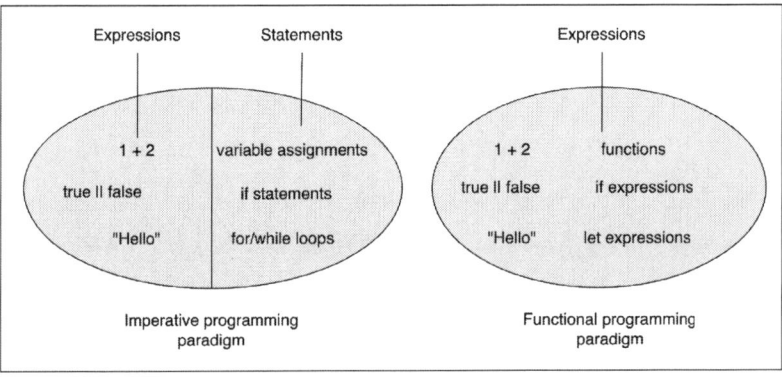

Figure 7: Language elements in imperative and functional programming

No wonder functional programming can feel odd for the uninitiated. It requires us to unlearn statements entirely. Since everything is an expression in the functional paradigm, a central part of learning a functional programming language is learning how to construct expressions and combine them to build larger ones. We'll discuss arithmetic, boolean, and string expressions in OCaml. Next, we'll discuss if expressions, functional programming's alternative to if statements in imperative programming languages.

2 EXPRESSIONS – BUILDING BLOCKS OF FUNCTIONAL PROGRAMS

2.1.1 Arithmetic expressions

OCaml provides built-in literal values for integer numbers, such as 1 and 2. Those literal values are often termed primitive expressions because they represent the simplest possible expressions.

OCaml provides built-in operators: +, -, *, / and mod. These are used to add, subtract, multiply, divide, and calculate the remainder of two integers. We can build compound expressions with the operators.

```
(* OCaml *)
1 + 2
```

Here, 1 and 2 are called operands. The + operator is called a binary operator because it accepts two operands. Compound expressions, in turn, can be used as operands, allowing us to construct arbitrarily complex arithmetic expressions. For example,

```
(* OCaml *)
(1 + 2) * (3 - 4 * 5)
```

OCaml provides dedicated operators for float numbers. To add, subtract, multiply, and divide float numbers, we use +., -., *., and /.

```
(* OCaml *)
3.14 *. 2.0 *. 2.0
```

Note that in OCaml, we can write 2. instead of 2.0 That means the expression above can be rewritten as

```
(* OCaml *)
```

2 EXPRESSIONS – BUILDING BLOCKS OF FUNCTIONAL PROGRAMS

```
2  3.14 *. 2. *. 2.
```

2.1.2 Boolean expressions

OCaml also provides comparison operators, such as =, >, >=, <, and <= for comparing two expressions. For example:

```
1  (* OCaml *)
2  1 = 2
3
4  (1 + 2) * (3 - 4 * 5) > 6 + 7
```

Comparison operators construct boolean expressions that evaluate to **true** or **false**. We combine boolean expressions with each other using logical operators not (negation), && (AND), and || (OR). For example:

```
1  (* OCaml *)
2  true && (1 > 2)
3
4  ((1 + 2) * (3 - 4 * 5) = -51) || (1 > 2)
5
6  not (true && (1 > 2))
```

Of course, there is no limit to how deeply those boolean expressions can be nested. Also notice that while most operators we have seen are binary, not exemplifies what is called a unary operator because it accepts only one operand.

2 EXPRESSIONS – BUILDING BLOCKS OF FUNCTIONAL PROGRAMS

2.1.3 String expressions

Like most programming languages, string literals in OCaml such as `"Hello"` are put inside quotes. We can use the `^` operator to concatenate two strings in OCaml.

```
1  (* OCaml *)
2  "Hello " ^ "FP"
3  (* Result: "Hello FP"*)
```

2.1.4 If expressions

One crucial aspect of any powerful programming language is testing a condition and choosing alternative computations depending on the result. Imperative programming languages provide the `if` statement used to express "if something is true, do this, or else do that." The following Java code shows a typical use of the `if` statement to calculate the maximum of two numbers, a and b.

```
1  // Java
2  if (a > b) {
3      max = a;
4  } else {
5      max = b;
6  }
```

As you can see, the `max` variable is updated depending on the condition. But in the functional paradigm, `if` is an expression of the form `if e1 then e2 else e3`. The right way of thinking is that if `e1` evaluates to `true`, the result is the value of the expression `e2`. Else, the result is the value of the expression `e3`. For example:

2 EXPRESSIONS – BUILDING BLOCKS OF FUNCTIONAL PROGRAMS

```
(* OCaml *)
if 1 > 2 then 1 else 2
```

The `else` branch in OCaml's `if` expression is mandatory because the entire `if` is treated as an expression, meaning it has to evaluate to a value regardless of the condition's outcome.

Since the condition and the two branches, `then` and `else`, may contain an expression, an `if` expression can be deeply nested that contains arbitrarily complex expressions, including other `if` expressions. For example:

```
(* OCaml *)
if 1 = 2 then if (1 + 2) * (3 - 4 * 5) = -51
    then 100 / 6 else 5 - 1 else 42
```

The mental shift from `if` statements to `if` expressions is a first step towards understanding functional programming's worldview – everything is an expression.

2.1.5 The power of combination

Do you play Lego? Many kids and adults enjoy spending hours building houses, robots, and human figures from the Lego blocks. What makes Lego so compelling is that we can combine the same set of blocks in endless ways to build virtually anything, limited only by our imagination. The secret of Lego's incredible flexibility is actually quite simple. From a limited set of simple blocks, we can assemble them to build more complex blocks, which can be combined to create even more complex blocks, and so on and so forth.

2 EXPRESSIONS – BUILDING BLOCKS OF FUNCTIONAL PROGRAMS

Why does that have anything to do with the art of functional programming? Because the same magic applies to expressions! Indeed, functional programming languages like OCaml provide a limited set of primitive constructs to build primitive expressions. Like Lego blocks, primitive expressions can be combined endlessly to form more complex expressions.

The functional programming paradigm can tap into the full power of combination because it relies exclusively on expressions as the building blocks. However, in the imperative programming paradigm, the ability to combine is severely restricted because of the two divided worlds of expressions and statements discussed at the beginning of this section. Statements like variable assignments, `if` statements, or loops do not compose well with expressions.

Let's look at a concrete example of this. As we saw in the previous section, functional programming languages treat conditionals like `if 1 > 2 then 0 else 42` as expressions. Because of this, we can combine it with other expressions easily. For example, `if 1 > 2 then 0 else 42` can be used as an operand of the operator `+`.

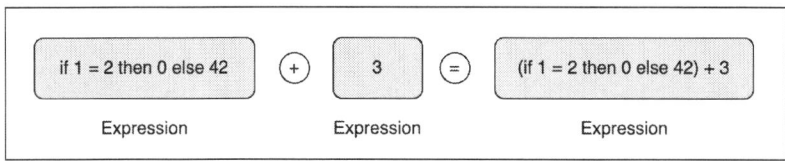

Figure 8: Combining if expression with another expression via '+' operator

2 EXPRESSIONS – BUILDING BLOCKS OF FUNCTIONAL PROGRAMS

However, we cannot do this in an imperative programming language where `if` is a statement rather than an expression. This example is admittedly tiny, but it shows that functional programming excels at composition by treating everything as expression.

2.2 Syntax of Expressions

At its core, a program written in any textual programming language, such as OCaml, Java and Python is nothing more than a long string consisting of characters we enter with a keyboard. A string that makes up a valid program in one programming language might be considered invalid in another and vice versa. To illustrate, consider the following obscure string:

```
1  ++++++++++[>+++++++>++++++++++>+++<<<-]>++.>+.
2  +++++..+++.>++.<<++++++++++++++.>.+++.------.
3  --------.>+.
```

Obviously, its not a valid OCaml program. The OCaml compiler will reject that string with a `syntax error` message. Yet, it is a valid Hello World program according to the esoteric programming language Brainfuck. Conversely, the string 1 + 2 is a perfectly valid OCaml program, but the Brainfuck compiler bluntly rejects it as invalid.

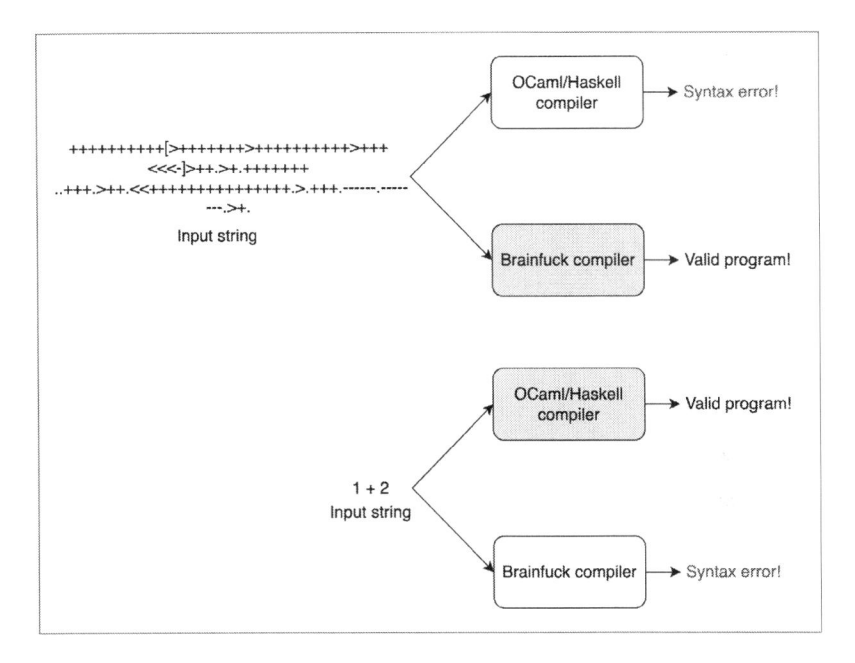

2 EXPRESSIONS – BUILDING BLOCKS OF FUNCTIONAL PROGRAMS

Figure 9: Example of languages interpreting the same string differently

The set of rules that define what input strings are considered valid programs is called the **syntax** of the language. In this section, we'll see how to specify those rules and apply them to define the syntax of OCaml expressions. The concepts introduced in this section are fundamental and they are also incredibly beneficial when you learn a new programming language. And we'll write tons of code soon, no worries!

With that out of the way, the best way to understand the syntax of programming languages is to draw an analogy from the syntax of natural languages.

2 EXPRESSIONS – BUILDING BLOCKS OF FUNCTIONAL PROGRAMS

2.2.1 Syntax of natural languages

Let's consider the syntax of the English language. The most primitive elements are alphabet letters, a, b, c, ..., x, y, z, A, B, ..., X, Y, Z. The letters are combined to form words. Of course, not all letter combinations are valid English words. For instance, "qpr" combines 3 English letters, q, p, and r, yet it is not a valid English word. On the other hand, "cat" is a valid English word.

English words represent the primitive expressive units of the language because they contain meanings. We put words, along with punctuation marks, such as commas, periods, and parentheses, together in sequential order to build phrases and sentences to communicate complicated concepts and ideas.

The following diagram visualizes how the English syntax is built up.

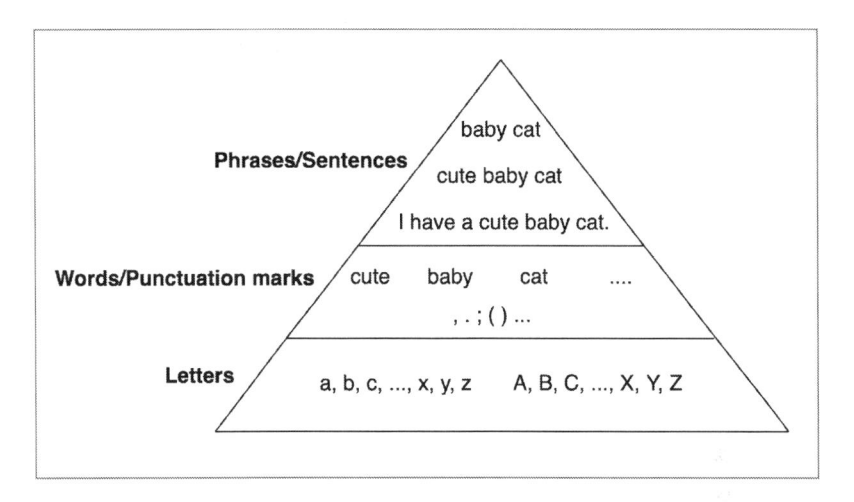

2 EXPRESSIONS – BUILDING BLOCKS OF FUNCTIONAL PROGRAMS

Figure 10: English syntax pyramid

The grammar of a natural language typically has a large set of rules specifying how to combine words. For instance, English grammar has rules that govern how **noun phrases** can be constructed. In particular, a noun phrase might be a single noun like "cat," or formed by placing an adjective before a noun, such as "cute cat." We can also combine a noun with a noun phrase to create a new noun phrase such as "baby cat."

We can use BNF, a very concise notation for codifying the syntax of a language, to specify the rules for English noun phrases.

```
1  <noun_phrase> ::= <noun>
2                  | <adjective> <noun_phrase>
3                  | <noun_phrase> <noun>
4
5  <noun> ::= baby | cat | dog | ...
6  <adjective> ::= cute | small | ...
```

2 EXPRESSIONS – BUILDING BLOCKS OF FUNCTIONAL PROGRAMS

Here, the bar symbol | indicates alternatives. Therefore, we can read the rules as "a noun phrase is either a noun, an adjective followed by a noun phrase, or a noun phrase followed by a noun."

Linguists have long recognized that expressive units of a language have hierarchical structures. For example, we can create a tree structure for the English phrase "cute baby cat" based on the rules above.

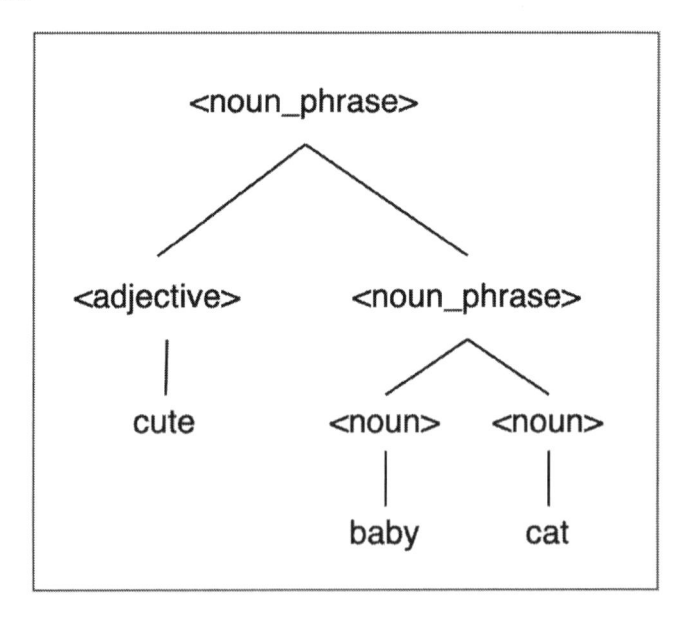

Figure 11: Tree structure of English phrase/sentence

Note that the tree structure captures our intuitive understanding that the two nouns, "baby" and "cat", form a noun phrase "baby cat" and the adjective "cute" describes this entire noun phrase.

2 EXPRESSIONS – BUILDING BLOCKS OF FUNCTIONAL PROGRAMS

2.2.2 Syntax of programming languages

The syntax of a programming language is built similarly to a natural language. In particular, the smallest elements are ASCII characters. They include alphabet letters a, b, c, …, x, y, z, A, B, C, …, X, Y, Z, and symbols +, -, (,), among others.

In the case of OCaml, the ASCII characters are then combined to form *literal values* (123, `true`, `"Hello"`), operators (+, >=), and *keywords* (`if`, `else`, `let`). We can think of them as "words" of the OCaml language. Just like how we combine English words into English phrases and sentences, we put together these OCaml "words" in sequential order to construct expressions. For example, the expression, 123 + 456, is formed by combining the literal number 123, the operator +, and 456 in that order.

The following diagram depicts how the OCaml syntax is built up, starting from ASCII characters all the way to expressions.

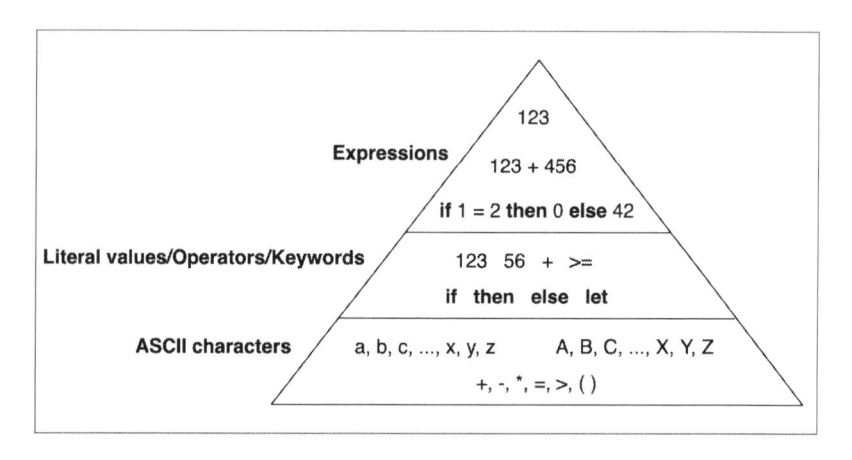

2 EXPRESSIONS – BUILDING BLOCKS OF FUNCTIONAL PROGRAMS

Figure 12: OCaml syntax pyramid

Like natural languages, OCaml has a set of rules that specify what sequences of literal values, operators, and keywords are valid OCaml expressions. We can use the BNF notation to specify the syntax of some of the OCaml expressions.

```
<expr> ::=
      | <number>
      | <unop> <expr>
      | <expr> binop expr
      | if <expr> then <expr> else <expr>

<number> ::= 0 | 1 | 2 | ...
<unop> ::= not | ...
<binop> ::= + | - | * | ...
```

The expressions we create following these rules have hierarchical structures. For example, the following diagram shows the tree structure of the expression, 1 + 2 * 3.

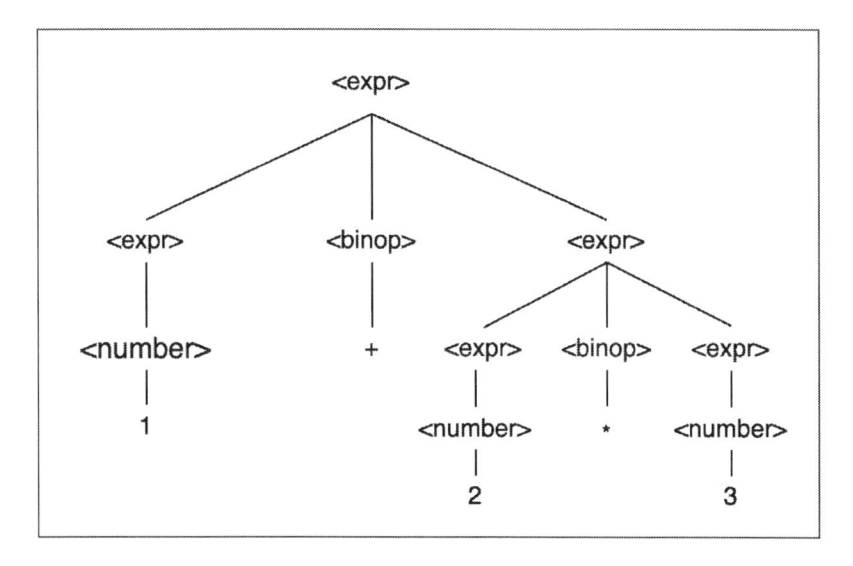

2 EXPRESSIONS – BUILDING BLOCKS OF FUNCTIONAL PROGRAMS

Figure 13: Tree structure of expression

The tree structure of the expression reflects the fact that multiplication * has higher precedence than addition +. That means 2 * 3 as a whole is the right operand of +.

The main takeaway from this section is that the role of the syntax of expressions specifies how characters and symbols are combined to make up valid expressions. Moreover, the syntax of an expression has a tree structure derived from applying the syntactic rules.

2.3 Parsing Expressions

The syntax of OCaml expressions consists of a set of rules that dictate what input string makes up a valid OCaml expression. Some of

2 EXPRESSIONS – BUILDING BLOCKS OF FUNCTIONAL PROGRAMS

the rules might look something like the following in the BNF notation.

```
<expr> ::=
    | <number>
    | <unop> <expr>
    | <expr> binop expr
    | if <expr> then <expr> else <expr>
    | ...

<number> ::= 0 | 1 | 2 | ...
<unop> ::= not | ...
<binop> ::= + | - | * | ...
...
```

Since the OCaml compiler implements all these rules, it can accept an input string as syntactically valid if it satisfies the syntactic rules. For instance, 1 + 2 follows the rule `<expr> binop <expr>` and is accepted by the OCaml compiler.

However, the OCaml compiler might reject input strings that do not follow its syntactic rules. For instance, the OCaml compiler will reject 1xyz + 2 with an error message:

```
Error: Line 1, characters 0-4:
Error: Invalid literal 1xyz
```

The error message indicates that the OCaml compiler cannot recognize 1xyz as a valid literal. Similarly, the OCaml compiler also rejects 1 + with an error message.

```
Error: Syntax error
```

This error message is different from the one above. While the former

2 EXPRESSIONS – BUILDING BLOCKS OF FUNCTIONAL PROGRAMS

ones say `Invalid literal`, the latter says `syntax error`.

In this section, we'll take a closer look at how the OCaml compiler does all these things through the process called parsing. We'll understand exactly why we got two different error messages in the examples above. Again, we'll draw analogies from natural languages like English.

2.3.1 How we recognize English sentences and phrases

Our ability to process natural languages is impressive. Looking at the letter combination "cute baby cat", we immediately know it's a correct English noun phrase. Equally intriguingly, we can tell quickly that "baby qbr cat" or "baby cute cat" is not a valid English phrase. How do we do that?

In its simplest form, we recognize the syntax of an English phrase/sentence in two stages

- Recognizing words
- Recognizing phrases/sentences.

The following diagram visualizes this process.

2 EXPRESSIONS – BUILDING BLOCKS OF FUNCTIONAL PROGRAMS

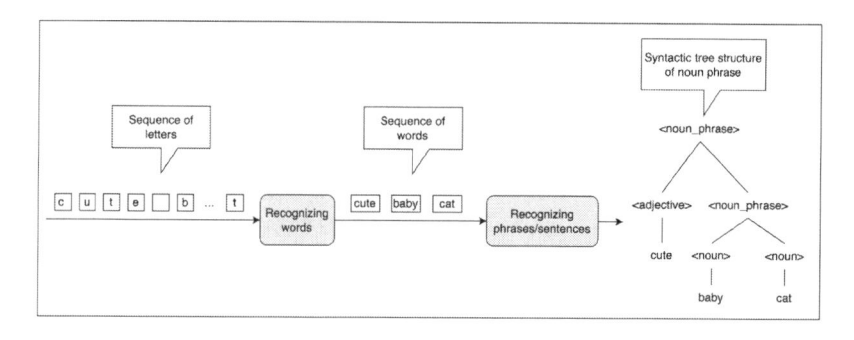

Figure 14: Process of recognizing an English phrase/sentence

The first stage is about recognizing words from a letter sequence. In our example, while scanning "cute baby cat" from left to right, we encounter the first letter "c". We keep building a letter combination until we reach the empty space. The first combination we obtain is "cute,"" which we recognize as a valid English word after looking it up in our memory or an English dictionary. Then we skip all empty spaces until we reach another non-empty space letter. The process of building another letter combination starts again. Upon reaching the end of the letter sequence, we'll have recognized 3 words "cute," "baby," and "cat." Of course, this stage might not go that smoothly. Suppose we encounter a letter combination that does not represent an English word, say "qpr" in the phrase "cute qpr cat." In that case, we stop and conclude that this is not a valid English phrase or sentence.

In the second stage, we check if the words are put together correctly to form a valid English phrase or sentence. We do this by mentally creating a tree structure based on the syntactic rules of English grammar. In our example, we recognize the word combination,

2 EXPRESSIONS – BUILDING BLOCKS OF FUNCTIONAL PROGRAMS

"cute baby cat," as a noun phrase.

2.3.2 Parsing process

The way a compiler of a programming language like OCaml processes an input string works similarly to how we recognize an English phrase or sentence. The compiler contains a component called a **parser** that is responsible for recognizing whether an input string is a valid program or not. This is known as the **parsing process**.

The parser goes through two stages, similar to what we described above with the English language. The following diagram shows how the OCaml parser recognizes the input string, `if 1 = 2 then 0 else` 42, as an `if` expression.

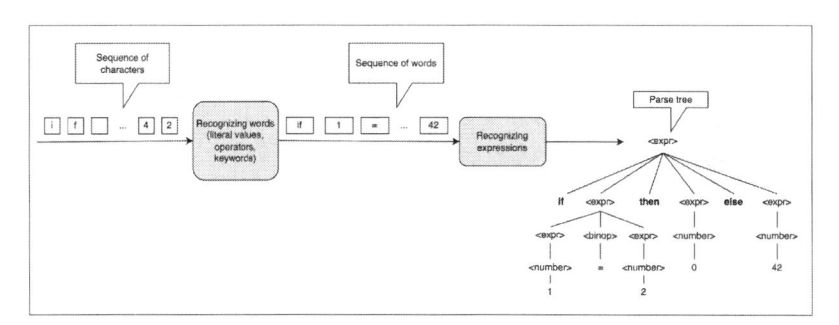

Figure 15: Process of recognizing OCaml expressions

In the first stage, the parser reads in a sequence of characters, i, f, , ..., 4, 2, and tries to recognize words (literal number, operators, or keywords). When reaching the end of the character sequence,

2 EXPRESSIONS – BUILDING BLOCKS OF FUNCTIONAL PROGRAMS

the parser recognizes `if` (keyword), 1 (number), = (binary operator), `then` (keyword), 0 (number), `else` (keyword), 42 (number). If, however, the parser encounters an invalid word, it rejects the input string and stops entirely. This is precisely what happens when the OCaml tries to parse `1xyz + 2`.

The error message, `Invalid literal 1xyz`, means that the parser can't recognize `1xyz` as a valid word of the OCaml language. This is very similar to how we can't recognize "qpr" as a valid English word.

In the second stage, the parser verifies that the words are put together in the correct order dictated by the OCaml grammar. The parser does this by trying to create a **parse tree** following the OCaml syntactic rules. In our example, the parse tree represents the syntactic structure of an `if` expression.

Of course, this second stage might not succeed either. If the combination of words does not follow the OCaml syntax, the parser rejects the input string. Recall when mentioned earlier that the OCaml compiler rejects `1 +` with the error message `Error: Syntax error`. Here, the OCaml compiler complains that the way words are put together does not satisfy the OCaml grammar. More specifically, the binary operator + requires two expressions as operands but the right operand is missing.

The parse tree for the expression, `if 1 = 2 then 0 else 42`, depicted in the diagram above looks quite complex for such a simple expression. To capture the essence of an expression, the parser usually creates a more compact tree structure called an

2 EXPRESSIONS – BUILDING BLOCKS OF FUNCTIONAL PROGRAMS

abstract syntax tree (AST). The term abstract refers to the fact that the tree merely shows an expression's structured content in which concrete details, such as whitespace, parentheses, or keywords are ignored. For example, a possible abstract syntax tree for the expression, `if 1 = 2 then 0 else 42`, is shown below.

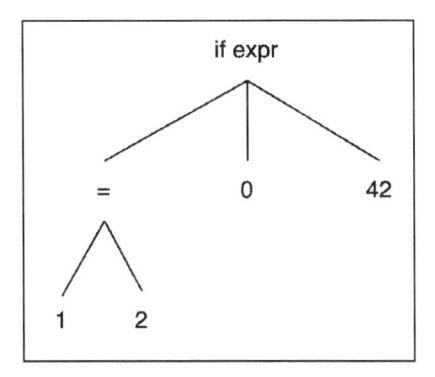

Figure 16: Possible abstract syntax tree (AST) of if expression

The compiler relies on the abstract syntax tree to further analyze the expressions, such as type checking or code generation into bytecode or native code.

An excellent way to grasp the role of the parser during the compilation process is that it reduces the set of all possible input strings to the set of syntactically valid expressions. The following figure illustrates this relationship.

2 EXPRESSIONS – BUILDING BLOCKS OF FUNCTIONAL PROGRAMS

```
Syntactically valid expressions        All possible input
   (accepted by parser)                     strings

           12 + 34
                                      1xyz + 2
       if 1 = 2 then 0 else 42
              ...                        1 +
                       ...

                           Syntactically invalid expressions
                               (rejected by the parser)
```

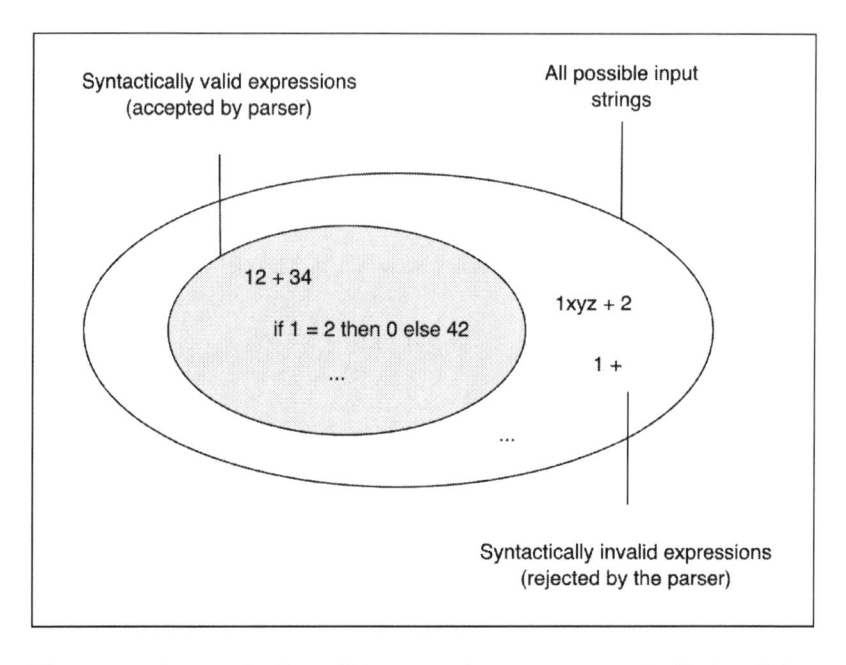

Figure 17: Syntactically valid expressions vs. syntactically invalid expressions

The innermost area represents the set of all syntactically valid expressions accepted by the parser. Conversely, all input strings outside the innermost area are syntactically invalid expressions and hence rejected by the parser.

2 EXPRESSIONS – BUILDING BLOCKS OF FUNCTIONAL PROGRAMS

2.4 Types of Expressions

2.4.1 Insufficient syntactic validation

Have you ever heard or read something that is syntactically correct but does not make any sense? We all have. Consider, for instance, the phrase "cute table cat." Syntactically speaking, it is a perfectly valid English noun phrase, but the meaning makes no sense, at least in real life. In particular, combining the noun "table" with the noun "cat" to form a noun phrase might perfectly follow the syntactic rules of English grammar. Yet, they don't seem to fit together from the semantic point of view.

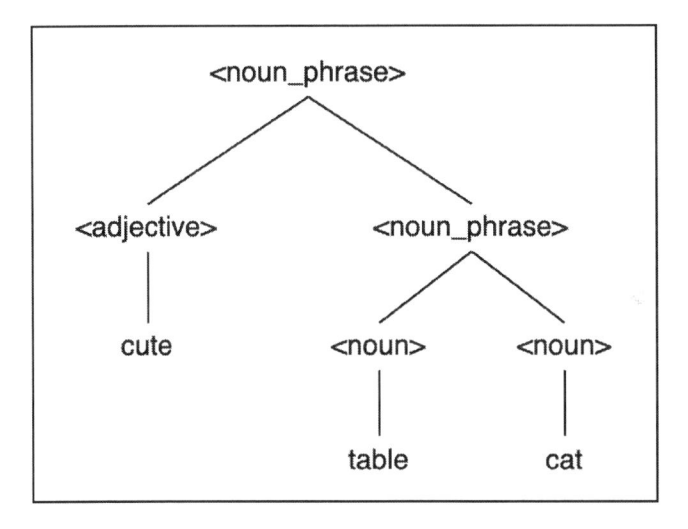

Figure 18: Syntactically valid, yet nonsensical English noun phrase

This applies to programming languages as well. We can construct syntactically valid programs that are nonsensical. Consider, 1 +

2 EXPRESSIONS – BUILDING BLOCKS OF FUNCTIONAL PROGRAMS

`true`, for instance. In most programming languages, it is a syntactically valid expression, formed by a binary operator + with two subexpressions, 1 and `true`, as operands. Yet, adding an integer with a boolean value generally does not make sense.

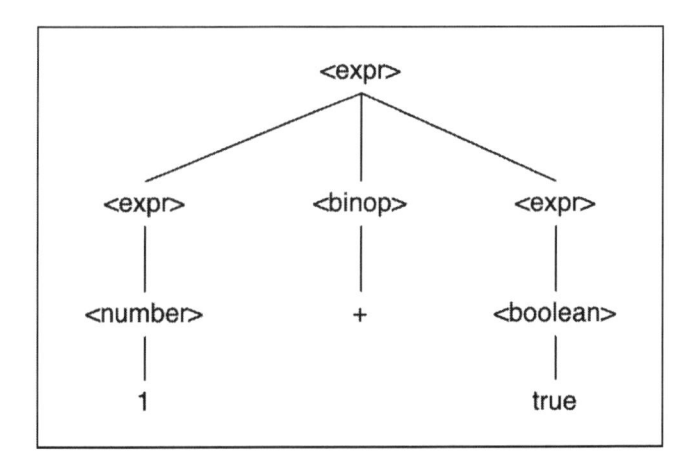

Figure 19: Syntactically valid, yet nonsensical expression

2.4.2 Dynamic typing vs. static typing

If you look at 1 + `true` closely, it's clear that there is a type mismatch in this expression. The binary operator + expects two operands of type numbers, but the right operand's actual type is boolean. When a type mismatch exists, we say that the expression does not type check.

How a programming language treats types hugely influences the expressivity of the language and how comfortable it is to program in the language. Many programming languages, notably JavaScript

2 EXPRESSIONS – BUILDING BLOCKS OF FUNCTIONAL PROGRAMS

and PHP, follow the so-called "dynamic typing" where type checking is not done during the compile time. For instance, the JavaScript interpreter gladly accepts 1 + true as a valid expression and executes it.

```
// JavaScript
console.log(1 + true)
// Result: 2
```

This JavaScript code is executable and the displayed result is 2. Why? Because JavaScript automatically converts true to 1. This might not be what the author of the code had in mind. While dynamic typing offers great flexibility, its biggest disadvantage is that many silly programming mistakes go uncaught and resurface only during the execution. Consider the following JavaScript code snippet.

```
// JavaScript
var x = 10;
console.log(x.length());
// Result: Uncaught TypeError: x.length is not
    a function
```

This program crashes at runtime because length is not a method provided by the type number. In larger programs, these kinds of errors can be tough to detect and debug.

In fact, this is the motivation behind Microsoft's TypeScript — a superset of JavaScript that adds static typing to mitigate some of dynamic typing's problems. Many functional programming languages, including OCaml and Haskell, are also statically typed. For instance, the OCaml compiler refuses to compile the expression, 1 + true,

2 EXPRESSIONS – BUILDING BLOCKS OF FUNCTIONAL PROGRAMS

because it does not type check.

2.4.3 Type checking

The OCaml compiler is equipped with a component called the **type checker**, responsible for checking the types of expressions. This process is known as **type checking**. During the compilation process, the type checker begins checking after the parser has successfully created an abstract syntax tree for the expression. The following diagram depicts the process from parsing to type checking.

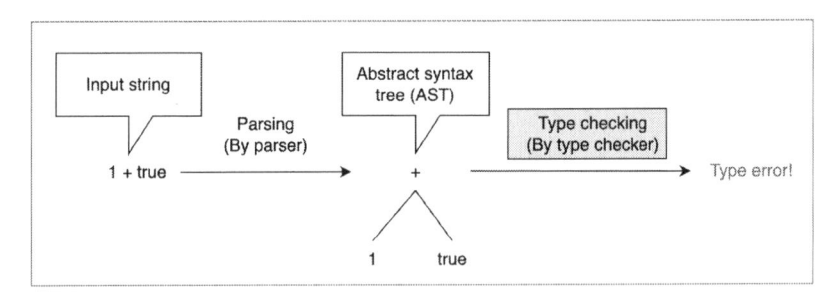

Figure 20: Parsing and type checking an expression

At its core, the type checker implements a type inference algorithm that can infer the type of any expression based on predefined typing rules. This way, expressions are classified according to their value type.

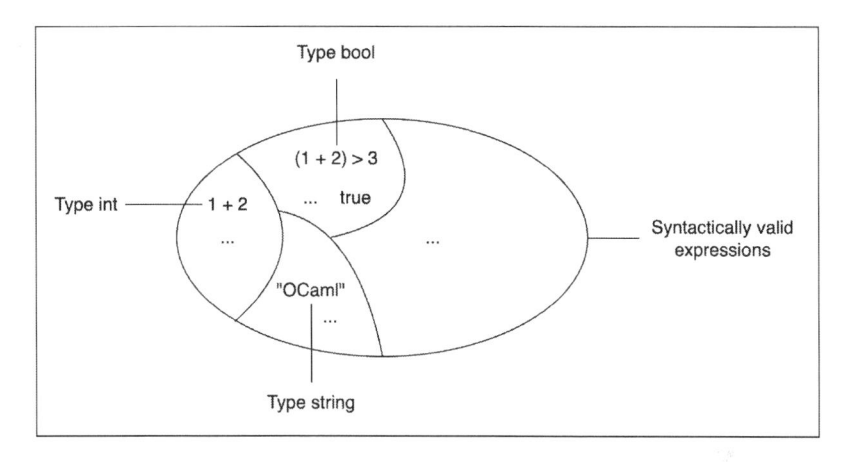

2 EXPRESSIONS – BUILDING BLOCKS OF FUNCTIONAL PROGRAMS

Figure 21: Classifying expressions according to types

Type inference is relatively straightforward. The following procedure deduces the types of some of the expressions we have discussed so far, following the recursive structures of expressions.

- Integers are expressions of the type `int`. Boolean constants, like `true` or `false`, are expressions of the type bool. String constants, such as `"FP"` or `"Lena"`, are expressions of the type `string`.
- Given unop is a unary operator accepting one argument of type t and returning a value of type t, and e is an expression of type t, then `unop e` is an expression of type t.
- Given binop is a binary operator accepting two arguments of type t1 and t2 and returns a value of type t3, and e1 and e2 are expressions of type t1 and t2, then `e1 binop e2` is an expression of type t3.

2 EXPRESSIONS – BUILDING BLOCKS OF FUNCTIONAL PROGRAMS

- Given e1 is an expression of type **boolean**, and e2 and e2 are of the same type t, then **if** e1 then e2 **else** e3 is an expression of type t.

Another way to look at this procedure is to propagate the types in the abstract syntax tree of an expression from the leaf nodes upwards until the root node type is deduced. The following diagram shows how the type of the expression, (1 + 2)> (3 - 4 * 5), is inferred.

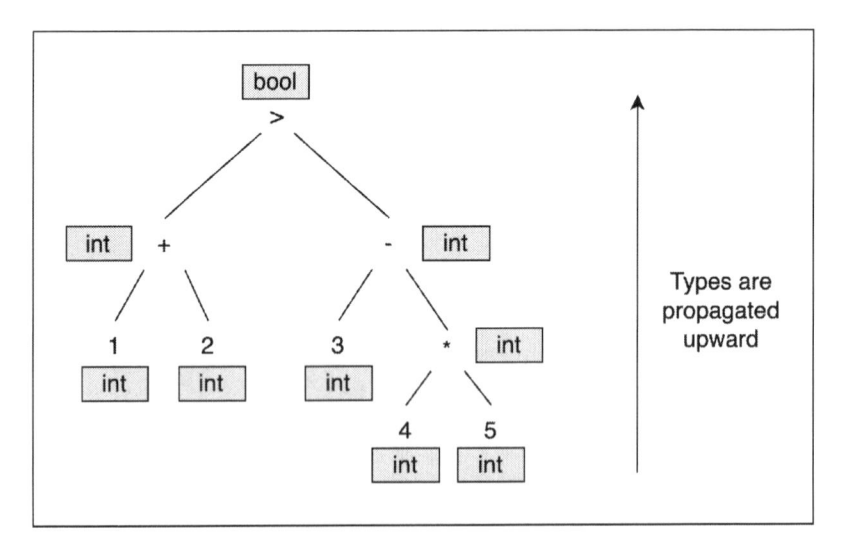

Figure 22: Propagating types upward in abstract syntax tree

Based on the type inference procedure, the type checker can easily detect type errors. For instance, in the case of 1 + **true**, the inferred type of the second operand is bool, which differs from the int type expected by the binary operator, +.

The Art of Functional Programming

2 EXPRESSIONS – BUILDING BLOCKS OF FUNCTIONAL PROGRAMS

Type checking an `if` expression is quite interesting. First, the type checker makes sure that the condition has the boolean type. For instance, the following `if` expression does not type check because the condition is a string, not a boolean type.

```ocaml
(* OCaml *)
if "Not bool" then 0 else 42
```

Moreover, in case the `if` condition has the boolean type, the type checker enforces that both `then` and `else` branches contain expressions of the same type. For example, the type checker produces an error message for the following `if` expression because there is a type mismatch between the two branches.

```ocaml
(* OCaml *)
if true 0 else "This is a string"
```

Let's stop for a moment and reflect on the role of the type checker in the OCaml compilation process. Out of all possible input strings, the parser accepts those that represent valid OCaml expressions. The type checker reduces the set of those syntactically valid expressions by only accepting those that do not contain any type errors. The following diagram illustrates this relationship.

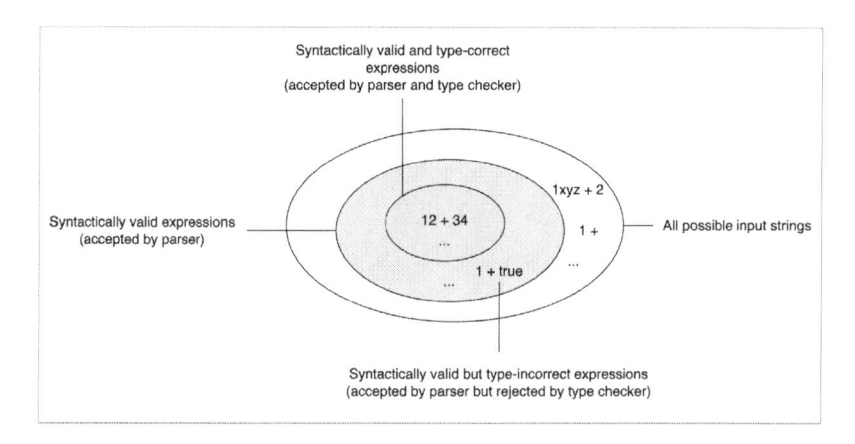

2 EXPRESSIONS – BUILDING BLOCKS OF FUNCTIONAL PROGRAMS

Figure 23: Parsing and type checking reduces the set of expressions

The innermost area represents the set of all syntactically valid expressions that type check, such as 12 + 34, accepted by both the parser and the type checker. Therefore, only expressions inside the innermost area are compiled and executed by the OCaml runtime. Conversely, the expressions outside the innermost area but inside the outer area, such as 1 + `true`, are syntactically valid. However, these are rejected by the type checker because they do not type check. As a result, these expressions do not even compile. The expressions outside of the blue area, such as 1xyz + 2, is syntactically invalid and rejected without ever reaching the type checker.

To summarize, programming languages with static typing such as OCaml and Haskell, provide a layer of security when we write programs. In particular, the type checker helps us avoid many common programming mistakes by telling us when there is a type mismatch.

2.5 Values of Expressions

2.5.1 Syntax vs. semantics

When studying languages in general and programming languages in particular, it is worth learning to differentiate between syntax and semantics. The syntax of a language specifies which character combinations are valid and which aren't. This section focuses on **semantics**, which is concerned with the meaning of those character combinations.

Consider, for instance, the expression 12 + 34. What we enter is nothing more than a string—a character combination – consisting of characters 1, 2, 3, 4, empty space, +, and so on. The OCaml parser recognizes this input, and creates an abstract syntax tree to represent the expression. Until this point, it's been all about syntax.

Now, an interesting question is, what about 46, the result of adding 12 and 34? This is the semantics of the string, 12 + 34.

The following diagram visualizes this distinction between syntax and semantics.

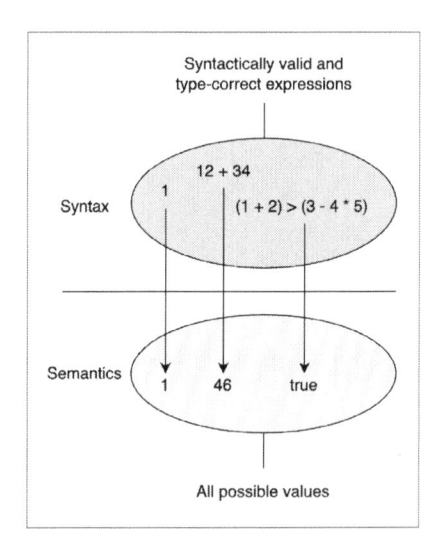

2 EXPRESSIONS – BUILDING BLOCKS OF FUNCTIONAL PROGRAMS

Figure 24: Mapping syntactic expressions to values

2.5.2 Interpret expressions

How does the runtime environment of a programming language evaluate the value of a given expression?

The answer to this question is a big decision made by programming language designers. There are two main classes of programming languages—interpreted and compiled. In the section, we'll discuss how interpreted programming languages **interpret expressions**.

At its simplest form, an interpreted programming language like JavaScript or Python has an interpreter that takes the abstract syntax tree of an expression and directly evaluates it.

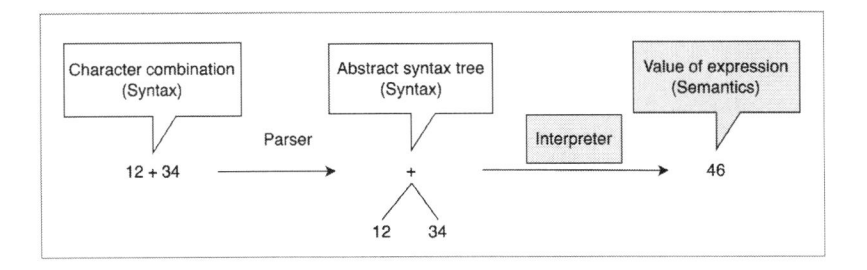

2 EXPRESSIONS – BUILDING BLOCKS OF FUNCTIONAL PROGRAMS

Figure 25: Interpreting an expression

The interpreter can evaluate an expression by following the expression's structure recursively:

- If the expression is primitive, such as a number, a boolean constant, or a string, it returns its value.
- If the expression is `unop e`, where `unop` is a unary operator, it evaluates `e` and applies `unop` to the result.
- If the expression is `e1 binop e2`, where `binop` is a binary operator, it evaluates `e1` and `e2` and applies `binop` to the results.
- If the expression is `if e1 then e2 else e3`, it evaluates `e1`. If the result is **true**, it evaluates `e2` and returns the result. Otherwise, it evaluates `e3` and returns the result.

Through the lens of an abstract syntax tree, the values are propagated from the leaf nodes up the tree until the value of the root node can be evaluated. The following diagram shows this process with the example of `(1 + 2)> (3 - 4 * 5)`.

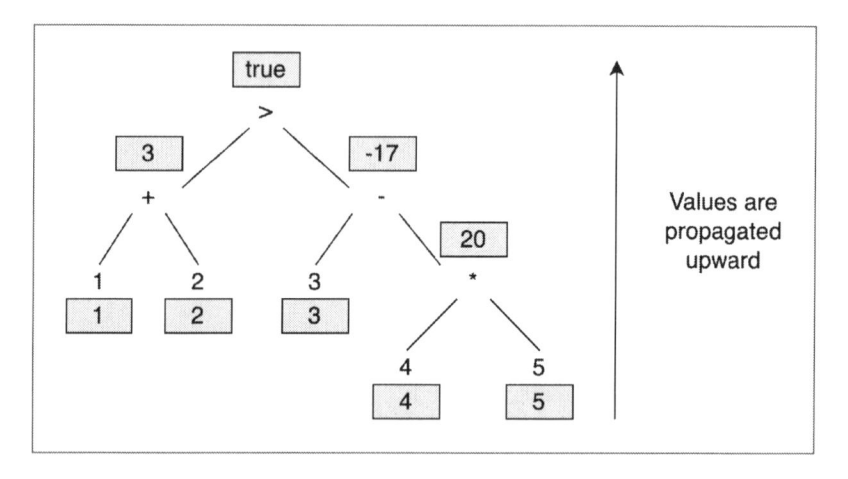

2 EXPRESSIONS – BUILDING BLOCKS OF FUNCTIONAL PROGRAMS

Figure 26: Evaluation of expression through the lens of abstract syntax tree

The procedure to interpret expressions closely resembles the type inference algorithm. This is no coincidence. Expressions have hierarchical structures and thus can be naturally processed by recursive algorithms.

2.5.3 Compile expressions and execute machine code

Unlike interpreted counterparts, **compiled programming languages** like OCaml, Haskell, and Java do not evaluate an expression directly. Instead, their compiler has a code generator component responsible for generating machine code - byte code or native code - from the abstract syntax tree of an expression. The byte code is executed by a byte code runner, while the native one can be executed by the CPU.

2 EXPRESSIONS – BUILDING BLOCKS OF FUNCTIONAL PROGRAMS

The following diagram depicts this approach.

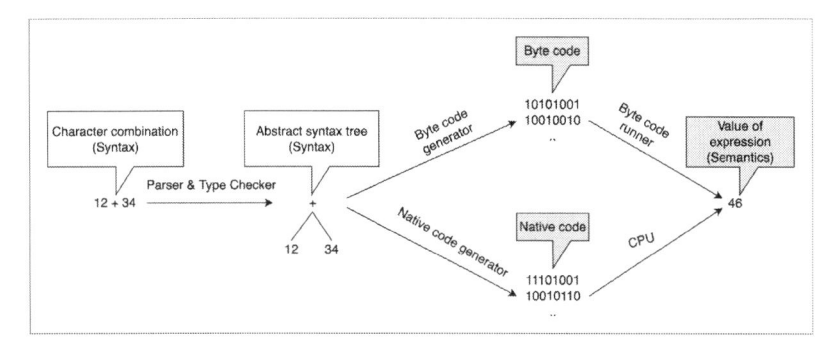

Figure 27: Compile expressions and execute machine code

OCaml provides a byte code generator, `ocamlc`. It also provides a native code generator, `ocamlopt`, to generate native code for various machine architectures.

The main point of this section is to peek into the process through which an input string is parsed and type checked, then either interpreted, or compiled and executed. A vital part of understanding this process is to know which parts are related to syntax and which are about semantics. This knowledge applies to all programming languages, not just OCaml. It comes in handy when we troubleshoot issues or learn new programming languages.

2.6 Assign Names to Expressions

Any powerful programming language has to provide the means for assigning names to computations. Consider, for example, the following OCaml expression.

2 EXPRESSIONS – BUILDING BLOCKS OF FUNCTIONAL PROGRAMS

```
1  (* OCaml *)
2  3.14 *. 2.5 *. 2.5
```

Without further context, it is not obvious what this expression tries to achieve. Now compare that with a new version where we associate those numbers with names.

```
1  (* OCaml *)
2  let pi = 3.14
3  let radius = 2.
4  let circle_area = pi *. radius *. radius
```

This code is much clearer. Anyone can recognize immediately that we are calculating the area of a circle with a radius, 2.0. Here, the `let` statement binds `pi` to 3.14 and `radius` to 2.0. These two names are used to calculate the circle area, which is then assigned to the new name, `circle_area`.

You might wonder "what's the difference between a name declared by `let` binding in a functional programming language and a variable in an imperative programming language?" Despite their similar appearance, they differ fundamentally from each other. In the following section, we'll look deeper into this difference.

2.6.1 Names as labels to memory cells

The imperative programming paradigm is centered around variables and variable assignments, or statements for updating variables. Consider, for example, the following Java code snippet to sum the squares of first n natural numbers.

2 EXPRESSIONS – BUILDING BLOCKS OF FUNCTIONAL PROGRAMS

```
1  // Java
2  int sum = 0;
3  for (int i = 1; i <= n; i++) {
4      sum = sum + i * i;
5  }
```

Here, we declare two variables, sum and i, that hold the program's state. We use a **for** loop to update those variables with variable assignments. A variable can be considered a memory cell to store data in the imperative programming paradigm. Moreover, the content of the cell might change over time. The name assigned to the variable acts as a label used to refer to that memory cell. The following diagram visualizes these labeled memory cells for our example.

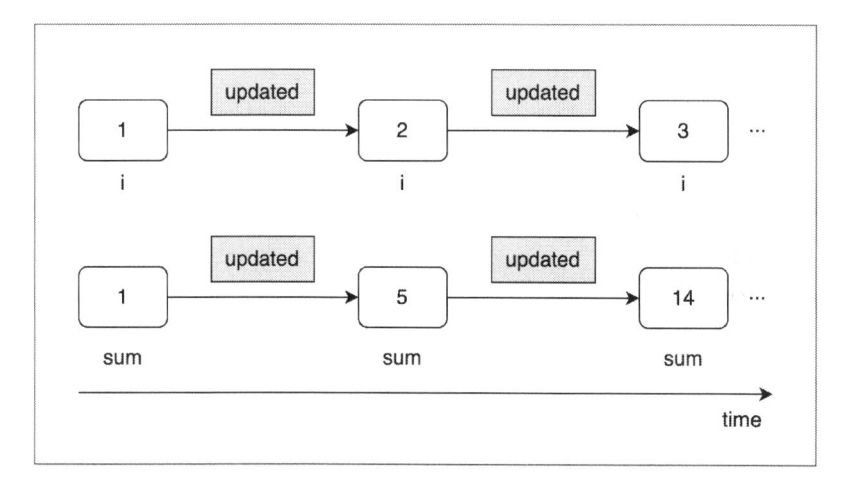

Figure 28: Names as labels of memory cells

We are used to this model of using names as labels of memory cells. This is because most of us picked up imperative programming as the first paradigm. However, this low-level thinking restricts our ability to think abstractly. We can't build a hierarchical structure of concepts with names when they are merely labels of memory cells. The functional programming paradigm promotes another much more powerful use of names – to create abstractions, which we'll look at in the next section.

2.6.2 Names as means of abstraction

Naming things is at the heart of human higher intelligence. It allows us to chunk information to overcome the limitation that human working memory can hold only a few items at a time. In his book *The Sense of Style*, Steven Pinker explains this chunking process with an easy-to-understand example. When we are a child and see someone give another a cookie, we remember it by the name "giving". When someone hands a cookie to someone else, and the other person gives back a banana in exchange, we call these two sequential acts "trading". One person can trade a banana to a second person for a medal because the second person can trade it to the third person for a cookie. We think of these acts as "selling" and "buying". When many people sell and buy, they form a "market". Activity in many markets is termed the "economy". And so on and so forth.

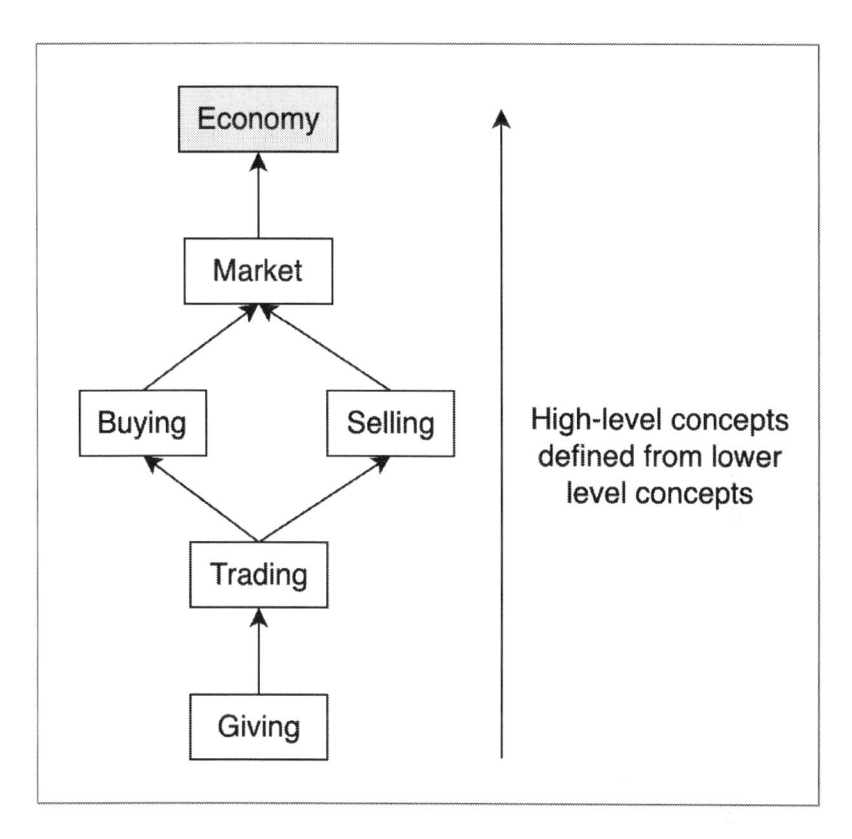

2 EXPRESSIONS – BUILDING BLOCKS OF FUNCTIONAL PROGRAMS

Figure 29: Names as means to create abstractions

Another way to look at this process is to use names to create abstractions. This is very powerful because it allows us to treat highly complex concepts as single units without caring about their details. For instance, we discuss or reason about the economy as if it was a single concept. We can even use it to form such a new concept as monetary policy. That is how the economy responds to actions by central banks.

2 EXPRESSIONS – BUILDING BLOCKS OF FUNCTIONAL PROGRAMS

What does this discussion have anything to do with functional programming? The answer is, this is precisely how we should think when assigning a name to an expression using the `let` binding in OCaml, Haskell, or any functional programming language. In the example of calculating the circle introduced at the beginning of this section, we can think of the naming process as building abstractions.

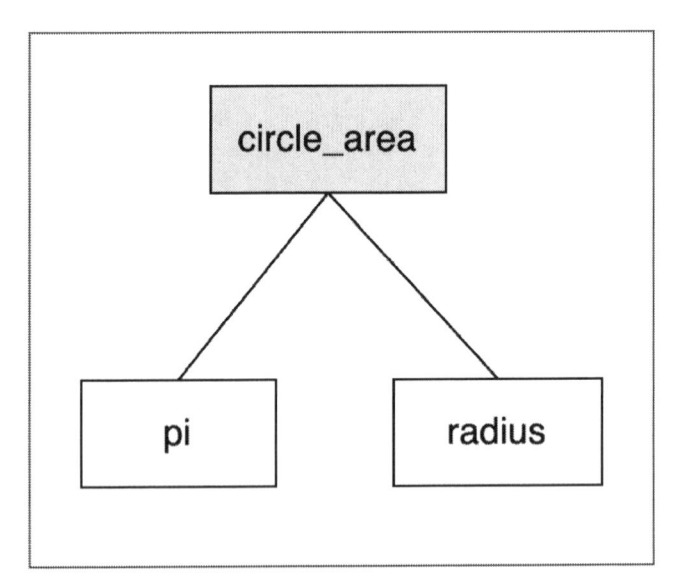

Figure 30: Build abstractions using names

When declaring `let pi = 3.14`, some people would say `pi` is an immutable variable, that is, a variable that can not be changed. Yet, it is best not to consider `pi` as a variable but as a name for a computation. Once `pi` is associated with the computation `3.14`, it becomes a self-contained concept. If we try to change the value of `pi`, we'll

2 EXPRESSIONS – BUILDING BLOCKS OF FUNCTIONAL PROGRAMS

see that the equal symbol, =, is reserved for comparing two values in OCaml.

2.6.3 Let in expressions

When we assign a name to an expression, such as `let pi = 3.14`, `pi` can be used in any expression that follows. We say that `pi` has the global scope. But often, a name should be used in only a particular context.

To illustrate, consider an example of human communication. Many years ago, in the first days of joining a company, I kept hearing colleagues say, "Let's have a telco tomorrow!" Quickly, I learned that "telco" refers to a kind of virtual meeting where team members from multiple locations can participate via telephones or computer software. The name "telco" creates an abstraction because it allows everyone to quickly communicate a particular kind of meeting as a single conceptual unit. What's noticeable about this term is that it has a local scope inside the company. Outside the company, the name is not very useful and better not used at all. The same thinking applies to programming.

Sometimes, we want to use a name in the context of a particular expression. This is precisely what `let in` is for. Consider our example of calculating the circle area. We can do the following if we want `radius` to be in the local scope of the formula to calculate the circle area.

```
1  (* OCaml *)
2  let pi = 3.14
```

2 EXPRESSIONS – BUILDING BLOCKS OF FUNCTIONAL PROGRAMS

```
3  let circle_area =
4      let radius = 2.0 in pi * radius * radius
```

Since `radius` is a local scoped name, it is invisible outside of the `let in`. Also, notice that `let in` is an expression because it evaluates to value. We can enhance our definition of expressions with `let in` expressions as follows:

```
1  <expr> ::=
2    | ...
3    | let <name> = <expr> in <expr>
```

The recursive definition means that `let in` can be arbitrarily nested. We can make use of this to define multiple names of local scope.

```
1  (* OCaml *)
2  let pi = 3.14 in let radius = 2. in pi *.
     radius *. radius
```

The main takeaway from this section is that we assign names to expressions to form abstractions in functional programming. This process closely resembles how we humans give names to new concepts to build up our knowledge.

2.7 Programming Challenges

Let's solve programming challenges related to expressions.

2 EXPRESSIONS – BUILDING BLOCKS OF FUNCTIONAL PROGRAMS

2.7.1 Challenge 1: Calculating max in functional style

The following imperative code calculates the maximum of three given variables by repeatedly updating `max_number`:

```
1  int x = 10;
2  int y = 2;
3  int z = 5;
4
5  int max_number = x;
6  if (max_number < y) {
7      max_number = y;
8  }
9  if (max_number < z) {
10     max_number = z;
11 }
```

Write this code in the functional style in OCaml.

2.7.2 Challenge 2: Calculating absolute value in functional style

The following imperative code calculates the absolute of a given variable using the variable assignment.

```
1  int x = -10;
2
3  int a = x;
4  if (x < 0) {
5      a = -x;
6  }
```

Write this code in the functional style in OCaml.

2.8 Solutions to Programming Challenges

2.8.1 Challenge 1: Calculating max in functional style

Recall that the functional programming paradigm does not have the concept of updating variables. Therefore, we do not try to update `max_number` in a sequence of variable assignments as with the imperative version. Instead, we define an expression that evaluates to the maximum.

```
1  (* OCaml *)
2  let max_number = let m = if x > y then x else
       y in if m > z then m else z
```

2.8.2 Challenge 2: Calculating absolute value in functional style

The absolute value of x is x if x >= 0 and -x otherwise.

```
1  (* OCaml *)
2  let a = if x >= 0 then x else -x
```

2.9 Quiz on Expressions

Let's test your understanding of expressions.

2 EXPRESSIONS – BUILDING BLOCKS OF FUNCTIONAL PROGRAMS

2.9.1 Quiz 1

Which of the following typical language elements of imperative programming languages do not exist in functional programming languages?

Please select all following choices that apply.

Choice A: Functions

Choice B: Variable assignments, such as `c = c + 1`

Choice C: `for/while` loops

2.9.2 Quiz 2

Given the following name declaration in OCaml

```
1  (* OCaml *)
2  let x = 42
```

What does `x = x + 1` do?

Please select all following choices that apply.

Choice A: It is a boolean expression that evaluates to `false`

Choice B: It increases the value of x by 1. So, x becomes 43.

2.9.3 Quiz 3

For the input `if true then 42 else "Bye"`, the OCaml compiler gives the following error:

2 EXPRESSIONS – BUILDING BLOCKS OF FUNCTIONAL PROGRAMS

```
1  Error: This expression has type string but an
       expression was expected of type
2           int
```

What kind of error is this?

Please select all following choices that apply.

Choice A: Syntax error

Choice B: Type error

2.9.4 Quiz 4

For the input, `if 00aa = 0 then "Hi" else "Bye"`, the OCaml compiler shows the following error:

```
1  Error: Invalid literal 00aa
```

What kind of error is this?

Please select all following choices that apply.

Choice A: A syntax error

Choice B: A type error

2.9.5 Quiz 5

What is the value of the following OCaml expression?

```
1  (* OCaml *)
2  let s = if 42 mod 2 = 0 then "even" else "odd"
       in "The number is " ^ s
```

2 EXPRESSIONS – BUILDING BLOCKS OF FUNCTIONAL PROGRAMS

Please select all following choices that apply.

Choice A: "The number is odd"

Choice B: "The number is even"

2.9.6 Quiz 6

What is the type of the following OCaml expression?

```
1  (* OCaml *)
2  let s = if 1 > 2 then "a" else "b" in (String.
        length s) > 0
```

Here, `String.length` is an OCaml function that returns the length of a string.

Please select all following choices that apply.

Choice A: `int`

Choice B: `bool`

Choice BC: `string`

2.9.7 Quiz 7

Given the following OCaml code

```
1  let a = 42
2  let b = let a = 1 in a + 1
```

What are the values of `a` and `b`?

Please select all following choices that apply.

The Art of Functional Programming

Choice A: a = 1 and b = 2

Choice B: a = 42 and b = 2

Choice C: a = 1 and b = 43

2.9.8 Quiz 8

Given the following imperative code in Java

```
// Java
int x = 1;

if (x >= 0) {
    x = x + 1;
} > 2
```

Why does the Java compiler reject this code?

Please select all following choices that apply.

Choice A: `if` is a statement and can not be used as an operand of the comparison operator.

Choice B: The parentheses are missing.

2.10 Answers to Quiz on Expressions

2.10.1 Quiz 1

Choice B and C are correct. Functional programming languages do not have variable assignments. Moreover, functional programming languages do not need `for`/`while` loops but rely on recursion for repeated computations.

2 EXPRESSIONS – BUILDING BLOCKS OF FUNCTIONAL PROGRAMS

2.10.2 Quiz 2

Choice A is correct. Here, `x = x + 1` compares two operands. The left operand's value is 42 while the right's value is 43. As a result, the entire boolean expression's value is `false`.

In general, functional programming does not have the concept of variables, which can hold different values over time. Instead, once a name is assigned to an expression, it cannot change to another expression. It is best to think of the name as an abstraction that refers to an expression as a conceptual unit. This is very similar to how we humans name things to extend our body of knowledge.

2.10.3 Quiz 3

Choice B is correct. The input string forms a syntactically valid expression according to the OCaml grammar. Yet, the OCaml compiler refuses to compile it because of type errors. In particular, the type checker enforces that the two branches of an `if` expression must have the same type. But in this expression, one branch is of type `int` while the other is a `string`.

2.10.4 Quiz 4

Choice A is correct. The error message says that the OCaml compiler cannot recognize the character combination `00aa` as a valid "word" according to the OCaml syntax.

2 EXPRESSIONS – BUILDING BLOCKS OF FUNCTIONAL PROGRAMS

2.10.5 Quiz 5

Choice B is correct. Since 42 is an even number, the value of s is "even". The value of the entire expression is the concatenation of "The number is" and the value of s.

2.10.6 Quiz 6

Choice B is correct.

2.10.7 Quiz 7

Choice B is correct. In the second line, a has a local scope in the expression `let b = ....` Since the value of the local scoped a is 1, b equals 2. The global scoped a is still 42.

2.10.8 Quiz 8

Choice A is correct. Statements like `if` in Java do not evaluate to values and can not be used as operands in other expressions.

3 Building Abstractions with Functions

3.1 Lambda Calculus: Foundation of Functional Programming

Functional programming is based on a theoretical foundation called lambda calculus (also written as λ-calculus), invented by Alonzo Church. The easiest way to understand lambda calculus is to think of it as an idealized bare-bones functional programming language. In other words, take OCaml or any similar functional programming language and strip down all features that do not contribute to the ability to do functional programming. What remains is essentially lambda calculus.

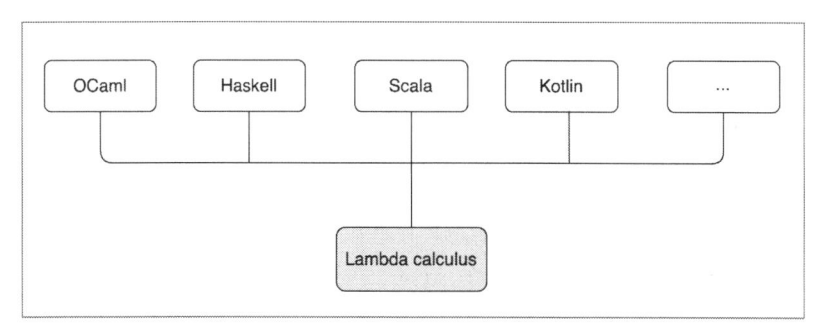

Figure 31: Lambda calculus as foundation for functional programming languages

3.1.1 Lambda expressions

The expressions of lambda calculus called lambda expressions, can be built from either one of the following three rules:

3 BUILDING ABSTRACTIONS WITH FUNCTIONS

- A variable x, y, myvar, etc., is a lambda expression.
- Given x is a variable and e is a lambda expression. A function abstraction $\lambda x.\, e$ is a lambda expression.
- If e1 and e2 are lambda expressions, a function application e1 e2 is also a lambda expression.

We can use the Backus–Naur form (BNF) notation to express the formal syntax of lambda calculus more succinctly.

```
1  <var> ::= x | y | myVar | ...
2  <lambda_expr> ::=
3      <var>
4    | λ <var> . <lambda_expr>
5    | <lambda_expr> <lambda_expr>
```

Moreover, we can use parentheses in lambda expressions to avoid ambiguity.

As we can see, lambda calculus centers around two concepts, function abstraction and function application, drawn directly from mathematical functions. **Function abstraction** formulates the way we declare a mathematical function of one argument, for example, $f(x) = x$. Likewise, in lambda calculus, $\lambda x.\, x$ represents a function that takes an input x and returns itself. This is the identity function. Function application resembles how we apply a function to an argument. For instance, we can apply $f(x) = x$ to 2 and obtain $f(2) = 2$. Similarly, $(\lambda x.\, x)\, y$ represents the act of applying the function $\lambda x.\, x$ to y.

Despite having only variables and functions as language elements, lambda calculus is as powerful as any general-purpose program-

3 BUILDING ABSTRACTIONS WITH FUNCTIONS

ming language, such as C, Python, Java, and OCaml. In particular, lambda calculus is powerful enough to encode and implement operations for numbers, boolean values, and data structures like pairs and lists. Read about Church encoding for more details. In fact, we could even write a microservice in lambda calculus! Admittedly, the code would likely look dreadfully complicated.

3.1.2 Lambda reduction

To run a program means to reduce the lambda expression denoting the program until the expression can not be further reduced. The fully reduced expression is the value of the program. A function abstraction such as $\lambda x.\, x\, x$ or a variable x is fully reduced. Conversely, a function application of the form $(\lambda x.\, e1)\, e2$ can be reduced further by substituting the function's formal argument x with the actual argument e2 into the function body e1. Such a lambda expression is called a reducible expression or redex.

For example,

$(\lambda x.\, x\, x)\, y$

$y\, y$

Now an interesting question arises, "Can we fully reduce any lambda expression in a finite number of steps?" The answer is no. There are lambda expressions that can never be fully reduced, $(\lambda x.\, x\, x)\, (\lambda x.\, x\, x)$ is one. This function application evaluates to itself.

$(\lambda x.\, x\, x)\, (\lambda x.\, x\, x)$

The Art of Functional Programming

3 BUILDING ABSTRACTIONS WITH FUNCTIONS

$(\lambda x.\, x\, x)\, (\lambda x.\, x\, x)$

$(\lambda x.\, x\, x)\, (\lambda x.\, x\, x)$

...

If you think about it, this makes a lot of sense. Lambda calculus allows us to formulate undefined values in the same way we can write Java or Python programs that run in an endless loop.

3.1.3 Functions are first-class citizens

One fascinating aspect of lambda calculus is that there is no distinction between a variable and a function – both are expressions. Variables or functions can be freely passed as an argument to another function or returned from another function. For example, $(\lambda x.\, x\, z)\, (\lambda y.\, y)$ represents a function application in which we apply the function $\lambda x.\, x\, z$ to the function $\lambda y.y$. Functions are said to be first-class citizens in lambda calculus.

Functional programming languages are built on this idea and treat functions as first-class citizens. In these languages, functions can be assigned to variables, passed to functions, or returned from functions like we usually do with numbers, boolean values, or strings. In contrast, in imperative programming languages, functions are second-class citizens. That means functions can't be used to construct expressions. We can neither assign functions to variables nor pass functions as arguments to other functions.

The concept of first-class citizens is one of the big ideas of functional programming. It is the foundation for higher-order functions, a hallmark of functional programming.

3.1.4 Currying and partial application

You might be surprised that lambda calculus only allows functions to have exactly one argument. How about functions with multiple arguments? A great insight of lambda calculus is that we can represent a multi-argument function as a chain of nested single-argument functions, a technique known as currying. The term is named after the logician Haskell Brooks Curry whose first name Haskell is also used to call a popular functional programming language.

To illustrate, suppose we want to formulate a function that accepts two arguments, x and y, then applies a function f to them, and returns the result. Using currying, we can define it as a chain of two single-valued functions, $\lambda x.\lambda y.\ f\ x\ y$.

Since $\lambda x.\lambda y.\ f\ x\ y$ is actually two nested functions, applying it to two arguments u and v means we first apply it to u and then v.

$(\lambda x.\lambda y.\ f\ x\ y)\ u\ v$

$(\lambda y.\ f\ u\ y)\ v$

f u v

Another fascinating aspect of currying is that it enables **partial application**. We don't have to apply the function, $\lambda x.\lambda y.\ f\ x\ y$, to two arguments. Instead, we partially apply it to a single argument, u, and stop entirely. What we obtain is a unary function $(\lambda y.\ f\ u\ y)\ v$, where we fix the variable x with u.

Currying together with partial application is another big idea of functional programming. OCaml and Haskell rely on currying to represent multi-argument functions.

3.1.5 Reduction strategies

We previously saw that a lambda expression of the form $(\lambda x\ e1)\ e2$ is a redex, reducible expression. But what if the argument $e2$ is also a redex? For example, $(\lambda x.\ x\ x)\ ((\lambda y.\ z)\ u)$ is itself a redex but the argument $(\lambda y.\ z)\ u$ is also a redex.

We could use either of the following two strategies:

- We reduce the argument $e2$ first and then substituting x with the fully reduced $e2$ in $e1$. This reduction strategy is often termed **call-by-value**.

- We substitute x with the entire expression g as is. This reduction strategy is also known as **call-by-name**.

The following compares these two strategies.

Call-by-value: Reduce the argument and then substituten

$(\lambda x.\ x\ x)\ ((\lambda y.\ y)\ z)$

$(\lambda x.\ x\ x)\ z$

$z\ z$

Call-by-name: Substitute the argument without reducing it

3 BUILDING ABSTRACTIONS WITH FUNCTIONS

$(\lambda x.\, x\, x)\, ((\lambda y.\, y)\, z)$

$((\lambda y.\, y)\, z)\, ((\lambda y.\, y)\, z)$

$z\, ((\lambda y.\, y)\, z)$

$z\, z$

These reduction strategies result in a different order of evaluation. Still, they both terminate and arrive at the same value. In fact, when applied to the same expression, if both reduction strategies terminate they always produce the same result.

However, these reduction strategies might lead to different results if an expression contains an undefined value, for example, a non-terminating subexpression. Consider, for instance, the function application $(\lambda y.\, z)((\lambda x.\, x\, x)\, (\lambda x.\, x\, x))$. Here, we can think of $\lambda y.\, z$ as a constant function that simply ignores the input argument and always returns z. Then we apply this constant function to $(\lambda x.\, x\, x)\, (\lambda x.\, x\, x)$, which represents an undefined value because the expression can never be fully reduced.

The reduction of $(\lambda y.\, z)((\lambda x.\, x\, x)\, (\lambda x.\, x\, x))$ either never terminates or terminates with a value, depending on the reduction strategies,. This is shown in the following comparison.

Call by value

$(\lambda y.\, z)((\lambda x.\, x\, x)\, (\lambda x.\, x\, x))$

$(\lambda y.\, z)((\lambda x.\, x\, x)\, (\lambda x.\, x\, x))$

$(\lambda y.\, z)((\lambda x.\, x\, x)\, (\lambda x.\, x\, x))$

...

3   BUILDING ABSTRACTIONS WITH FUNCTIONS

Call by name

$(\lambda y.\, z)((\lambda x.\, x\, x)\, (\lambda x.\, x\, x))$

z

The expressiveness of a functional programming language largely depends on which reduction strategy it follows. OCaml and Haskell follow different strategies that lead to some fundamental differences.

3.2   Function Abstraction and Function Application

Lambda calculus, a model of computation based on functions, serves as the foundation for all functional programming languages. Not surprisingly, functions lie at the heart of the functional paradigm. In this section, we'll study how OCaml implements functions, especially function abstraction and function application. Most of what is described here works similarly to other functional programming languages, such as Haskell and Scala.

3.2.1   Function declaration

Recall that a function abstraction is defined using lambda λ in lambda calculus. The equivalence of λ in OCaml is the keyword, `fun`. For example:

```
1  (* OCaml *)
2  fun x -> x *. x
```

3 BUILDING ABSTRACTIONS WITH FUNCTIONS

Here, `fun` declares a function that takes `x` as a float argument and returns its square. We typically call `fun x -> x *. x` a function, focusing on the result itself rather than the abstraction process.

As with lambda calculus, functions are first-class citizens in OCaml. They are normal values that are treated no more differently than numbers, strings, or boolean values. In other words, a function is an expression that evaluates to a function value. The following diagram illustrates this:

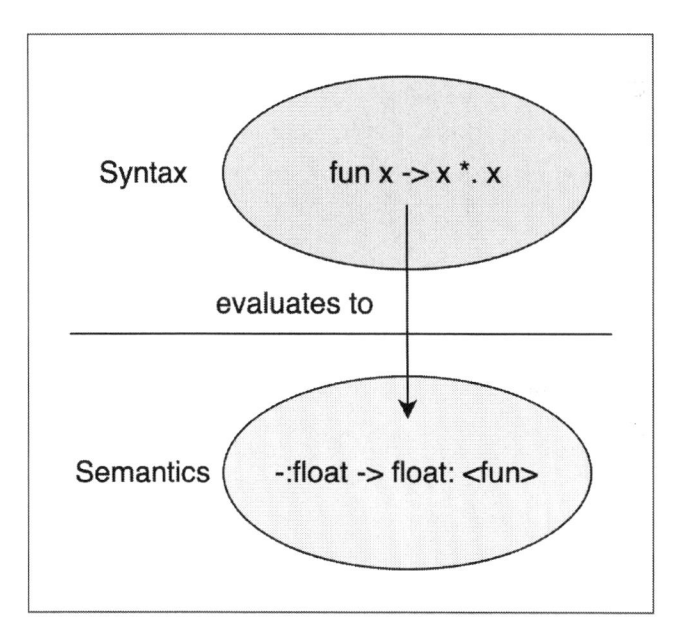

Figure 32: Lambda expression evaluates to a function value

In imperative programming languages, functions are not first-class citizens. Instead, they're second-class citizens and hence do not evaluate to values. For example, assume we define the following

3 BUILDING ABSTRACTIONS WITH FUNCTIONS

Java function:

```
// Java
double square(int x) {
    return x * x;
}
```

This Java function is treated differently from numbers, booleans, or strings. It does not evaluate to a value and we can't store it in a data structure.

Treating functions as first-class citizens is the hallmark of functional programming languages. This is the enabler for many essential functional programming techniques, such as currying and higher-order functions. A function formed with `fun` such as `fun x -> x *. x` does not have a name and therefore is often called an anonymous function, but also a lambda function, or an even arrow function in JavaScript. As a function is just a normal expression, we can assign a name to a function via the `let` binding as with any other kind of expression.

The following OCaml code snippet assigns a name to a function expression:

```
(* OCaml *)
let square = fun x -> x *. x
```

For the sake of convenience, OCaml provides syntactic sugar, that is, convenient syntax, to declare a named function that looks familiar to other programming languages.

```
(* OCaml *)
let square x = x *. x
```

3 BUILDING ABSTRACTIONS WITH FUNCTIONS

3.2.2 Function application

The syntax for function application in OCaml is identical to that in lambda calculus. In particular, we place a function and its argument next to each other, separated by a space. The following OCaml code applies the (fun x -> x *. x) function to an argument:

```
1  (* OCaml *)
2  (fun x -> x *. x) 2.
3  (* Result: 4. *)
```

Conceptually, function application in OCaml is also based on substitution, like in lambda calculus. In our example, the evaluation of (fun x -> x *. x)2. looks as follows:

(fun x -> x * x)2.

2. *. 2.

4.

Things become more interesting when the argument is not fully reduced. What does the evaluation of (fun x -> x *. x)(1. +. 2.) look like? Would (1. +. 2.) be evaluated first and then substituted into the function body or is the entire (1. +. 2.) argument substituted into the function body before the body is evaluated?

OCaml follows the call-by-value strategy. That means the argument is always evaluated first, before its value is used in the function body. In fact, call-by-value is the typical strategy employed by most mainstream programming languages, such as Java, C, or Python. Those languages are called strict languages.

3 BUILDING ABSTRACTIONS WITH FUNCTIONS

Haskell is one of the few programming languages to have non-strict semantics. In particular, it follows the call-by-name evaluation strategy wherein the argument is substituted as-is into the function body. To put it another way, an argument of a function application in Haskell is only evaluated if really needed.

The following comparison demonstrates how the difference in evaluation strategies leads to different execution.

OCaml is a strict language (it follows the call-by-value strategy)

```
(fun x -> x *. x)(1. +. 2.)
(fun x -> x *. x)3.
3. *. 3.
9.
```

Haskell is a non-strict language (it follows the call-by-name strategy)

```
(\x -> x * x)(1.0 + 2.0)
(1.0 + 2.0)* (1.0 + 2.0)
3.0 * (1.0 + 2.0)
3.0 * 3.0
9.0
```

Note that Haskell uses the backslash \ for function abstraction because of its resemblance to λ.

3 BUILDING ABSTRACTIONS WITH FUNCTIONS

In the example above, two different evaluation strategies result in the different order in which the subexpressions are evaluated. Yet, they both lead to the same value.

Looking at the comparison, we might be tempted to think that the call-by-value strategy is better. This is because the call-by-name strategy causes the argument, (1.0 + 2.0), to be evaluated twice, which is a waste. However, this strategy is advantageous when the argument of a function application is not used at all.

The following code snippet is an example of a function application in OCaml, whereby the argument is an expression that evaluates to an undefined value and yet is not used in the function body:

```
(* OCaml *)
let cons x = 42

cons (1/0)
(* Result: Division_by_zero *)
```

Running the code above will cause an `Division_by_zero` exception error. This is because the argument, 1/0, is evaluated even though it's not used.

Let's look at the same code in Haskell:

```
-- Haskell
cons x = 42

cons (1/0)
-- Result: 42
```

Unlike the OCaml version, cons (1/0) in Haskell returns 42 because the argument is not used anywhere in the function body and

The Art of Functional Programming

3 BUILDING ABSTRACTIONS WITH FUNCTIONS

thus never evaluated.

3.2.3 Function types

OCaml is a strong, statically typed programming language. This implies that every expression in OCaml is associated with a type. Since functions are expressions, they too can be classified into types. A function that takes an argument of the `t1` type and returns an output of the `t2` type has the type `t1 -> t2`, also called a function type. Since OCaml's type checker can infer a function's type based on its definition, we usually don't need to explicitly specify the function type.

For example, we previously defined the function `square` without stating its type.

```ocaml
(* OCaml *)
let square = fun x -> x *. x
```

The type checker is smart enough to infer the type of `square` as **float** -> **float**, meaning the function takes an argument of the **float** type and returns an output of the **float** type.

The primary use of function types is for the type checker to catch nonsensical function applications at compile-time. In the case of `square`, the only meaningful application of `square` is to an argument of the **float** type. Applying it to, say, a string would make no sense and hence be rejected by the type checker.

Since a function type has the form, `t1 -> t2`, a natural question

3   BUILDING ABSTRACTIONS WITH FUNCTIONS

arises, can `t1` or `t2` be function types themselves? For example, `int -> (bool -> string)`.

The answer is yes. We'll see this kind of function type more often when we talk about currying or higher-order functions in the next sections. For now, it's sufficient to say that `int -> (bool -> string)` represents a function that accepts an integer and returns a function, which in turn takes a boolean argument and returns a string. Of course, there are an infinite number of functions satisfying this function type. For example,

```ocaml
(* OCaml *)
fun x -> fun y -> if (x > 0) && y then "Hello"
    else "Good bye"
```

A general piece of advice is that it's usually a good idea to examine the function type when looking at a function. We do this because the type reveals the public contract of a function. Grasping this contract is often half the battle towards understanding what the function does and how to use it.

3.2.4 Functions as black box abstractions

To create abstractions capturing methods of computation, we declare and name a function. For instance, by defining the `square` function, we obtain a method to compute the square of any number, not just the square of a particular one.

3 BUILDING ABSTRACTIONS WITH FUNCTIONS

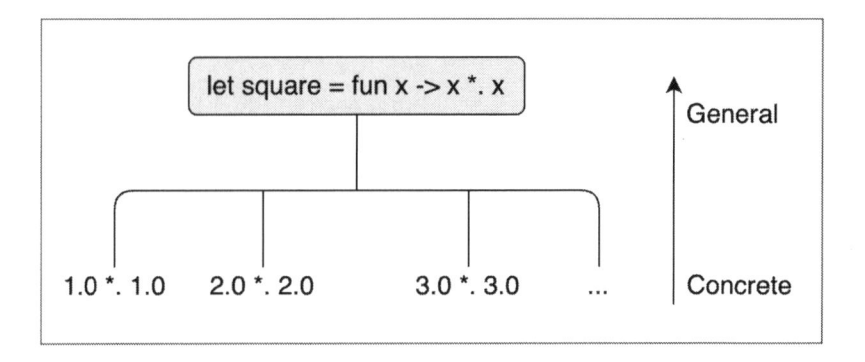

```
                  let square = fun x -> x *. x
                                                        ↑
                                                        │ General
                                                        │
  1.0 *. 1.0    2.0 *. 2.0      3.0 *. 3.0     ...      │ Concrete
```

Figure 33: Square as a method to compute the square of any number

Once `square` is defined, we can't differentiate it from OCaml's built-in functions like `mod` or operators `+` or `*`. We can use `square` as a building block to construct other functions, such as one that computes a given circle's area.

```
1  (* OCaml *)
2  let circle_area r = pi *. (square r)
3
4  circle_area 2.0
5  (* Result: 12.56 *)
```

The following diagram illustrates how `circle_area` is constructed from other functions:

3   BUILDING ABSTRACTIONS WITH FUNCTIONS

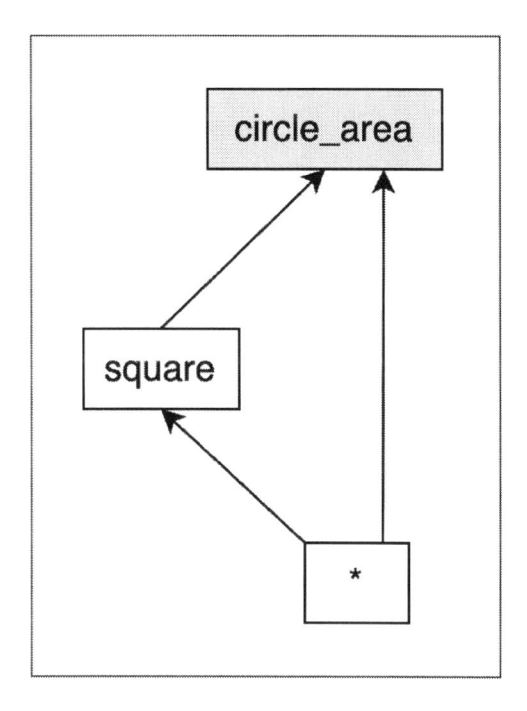

Figure 34: Constructing functions from other functions

The function, `circle_area`, becomes a new abstraction on its own, capturing a method to compute the area of a circle of any radius. In this example, `circle_area` plays the role of a client who uses `square`. From the client's point of view, it is irrelevant how the `square` function is implemented, as long as it fulfills its promise to square the argument. In other words, the client can treat a function as a black box.

3 BUILDING ABSTRACTIONS WITH FUNCTIONS

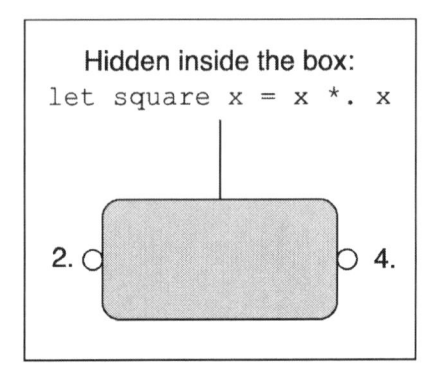

Figure 35: Function as a black box

The main takeaway is that one central aspect of functional programming is to stay alert to opportunities for abstractions hidden in computations that can be applied to arguments. Once we identify such a computation, we can formulate it as a function and give it a descriptive name. Then we can treat the named function as a self-contained concept and use it to construct even more functions capturing new abstractions. This allows us to build complex programs from simpler building blocks in a stepwise manner.

3.3 Use Currying for Function Chaining

3.3.1 Function with multiple arguments

One significant insight from lambda calculus is currying – we can formulate a function accepting multiple arguments as a nested chain of single-valued functions. Most functional programming languages, including OCaml, incorporate this technique into the language.

To illustrate, let's look at OCaml's built-in binary operator +, to add two integers. Internally, OCaml implements + as a normal function. Although we normally use + in the infix notation like 1 + 2, OCaml allows us to use + in the prefix notation by placing it in parentheses (+). That means, we can write (+) 1 2.

Except for its odd name, (+) is a normal function like any other function. It's a binary function that accepts two integers and returns their sum. Its type is `int -> int -> int`. Also, note that the -> operator is right-associative and so the type is equivalent to `int -> (int -> int)`. OCaml defines the addition operator + as a function that takes one integer argument and returns a function of type `int -> int`.

OCaml and most functional programming languages only implement built-in support for single-valued functions and rely on the currying technique to represent multi-argument functions. However, for the sake of convenience, those languages typically provide syntactic sugar to declare multi-argument functions. In particular, the `fun` keyword in OCaml also allows us to declare an anonymous function that accepts multiple arguments separated by spaces. For example:

```
1  (* OCaml *)
2  fun x y -> x * x + y * y
```

This is just a syntactic sugar for `fun x -> fun y -> x * x + y * y`.

Similarly, the `let` binding allows us to define a named function of multiple arguments using a familiar syntax. For example:

```
(* OCaml *)
let rectangle_area w h = w *. h
```

This definition is a syntactic sugar for `let rectangle_area = fun w -> fun h -> w *. h`.

3.3.2 Partial application

Currying allows us to apply a function to fewer actual arguments than the number of the function's formal arguments, a process known as **partial application**.

To illustrate, we previously defined a function to calculate a rectangle's area with a given width and height.

```
(* OCaml *)
let rectangle_area w h = w *. h
```

Due to currying, however, `rectangle_area` is actually a unary function that accepts a width `w` and returns another unary function. As a result, we can partially apply `rectangle_area` to just one argument.

```
(* OCaml *)
rectangle_area 2.
```

Here, we obtain a unary function of type `float -> float` that calculates the area of a rectangle whose width is fixed at 2.0, and whose

3 BUILDING ABSTRACTIONS WITH FUNCTIONS

height is provided as an input. In fact, we can even give this new function a name and use it like any other function.

The following code illustrates currying in action:

```
(* OCaml *)
let rectangle_area w h = w *. h
let rectangle_area_of_width_fixed_at_2 =
    rectangle_area 2.


rectangle_area_of_width_fixed_at_2 3.
(* Result: 6. *)
```

Partial application is very powerful because it enables us to reuse a multi-argument function for use cases the creator of the function may not have even thought of. For example, the built-in operator, +, is meant to calculate the sum of two integers. Thanks to partial application, we instantaneously obtain a function that increases its argument by 1 for free by adding (+) 1.

```
(* OCaml *)
let inc = (+) 1

inc 10
(* Result: 11 *)
```

The multiplication operator, *, can be used as a function by wrapping it around parentheses (*). The spaces are needed to avoid syntactic clash OCaml comments, (* This is an OCaml comment *). Using partial application, (*)2 is a function that doubles an input.

```
(* OCaml *)
```

3 BUILDING ABSTRACTIONS WITH FUNCTIONS

```
2  let double = ( * ) 2
3
4  double 10
5  (* Result: 20 *)
```

Currying and partial application imply that we need to change how we view function application to multiple arguments. Consider the following example.

```
1  (* OCaml *)
2  rectangle_area 2.5 3.5
```

If we were programming in an imperative programming language like Java, we apply `rectangle_area` to two arguments, `2.5` and `3.5`, at the same time. Yet in a functional programming language like OCaml, it's more appropriate to view the function application as consisting of two steps:

```
1  (* OCaml *)
2  (rectangle_area 2.5) 3.5
```

First, we apply `rectangle_area` to `2.5` and obtain a one-argument function. Next, we apply that one-argument function to `3.5` to get the final value.

This view of function applications comes in handy when we design a multi-argument function and decide how to arrange the arguments. Currying and partial application are at the core of functional programming languages. Non-functional programming languages like C or Java do not support these techniques.

3 BUILDING ABSTRACTIONS WITH FUNCTIONS

3.4 Recursive Functions

3.4.1 Where are the for/while loops?

If you are new to functional programming, you might be wondering, "How can I make a loop in a functional programming language?" Assume you want to calculate the sum, 1 + 2 + 3 + ... + n, for a given n natural number. In a non-functional programming language, we typically use a `for` or `while` loop:

```
// Java
int sum (int n) {
    int s = 0;
    for (int i = 1; i <= n; i++) {
        s = s + i;
    }
    return s;
}
```

This way of programming is inherently imperative because we explicitly specify the steps required to update s via variable assignment within a loop.

In the functional paradigm, however, we express sum as an expression. In particular, we can have a mathematical definition of sum as follows:

$$sum(n) = \begin{cases} 0, & \text{for } n = 0 \\ n + sum(n-1), & \text{for } n > 0 \end{cases}$$

We can translate this definition directly into a recursive function – a function that calls itself. Such a function is marked with the `rec`

3 BUILDING ABSTRACTIONS WITH FUNCTIONS

keyword in OCaml.

```
(* OCaml *)
let rec sum n = if n <= 0 then 0 else n + sum (n-1)

sum 3
(* Result: 6 *)
```

As you delve into functional programming, your thinking will soon shift from "How can I use a loop to compute this?" to "What is the recursive structure of the computation I'm trying to formulate?". The good news is, many computations in programming have inherently recursive structures, which makes them ideal to be formulated as recursive functions.

As powerful as recursion is, it is associated with an infamous problem – stack overflow. In our case, if we apply sum to a large number, the function execution might eventually reach the stack limit. If we calculate sum 1000000, we'll see a stack overflow exception.

```
(* OCaml *)
let rec sum n = if n <= 0 then 0 else n + sum (n-1)

sum 1000000
(* Result: exception Stack_overflow *)
```

Before discussing solutions for this issue, let's review why the stack overflow problem occurs in the first place. The following visualizes the process evolved from computing sum 5.

```
sum 5
5 + sum 4
```

3 BUILDING ABSTRACTIONS WITH FUNCTIONS

```
3   5 + (4 + sum 3)
4   5 + (4 + (3 + sum 2))
5   5 + (4 + (3 + (2 + sum 1)))
6   5 + (4 + (3 + (2 + (1 + sum 0))))
7   5 + (4 + (3 + (2 + (1 + 0))))
8   5 + (4 + (3 + (2 + 1)))
9   5 + (4 + (3 + 3))
10  5 + (4 + 6)
11  5 + 10
12  15
```

The shape of the process reveals that in the first half steps, the process consists of a chain of deferred calculations, which are then resolved in the second half steps. In particular, when we calculate sum 5, it tries to compute 5 + sum 4. Since sum 4 is unknown, the execution environment temporarily leaves sum 5 to execute sum 4, which equals computing 4 + sum 3. But sum 3 is also unknown, so the execution environment again has to temporarily leave sum 4 to execute sum 3 and so on. Each time the environment leaves a function execution to call another function, it pushes a stack frame on a call stack to remember where it should return later. The number of stack frames grows linearly with n. If it crosses a certain threshold, we get the stack overflow error.

The following diagram shows the call stack when executing sum 5.

3 BUILDING ABSTRACTIONS WITH FUNCTIONS

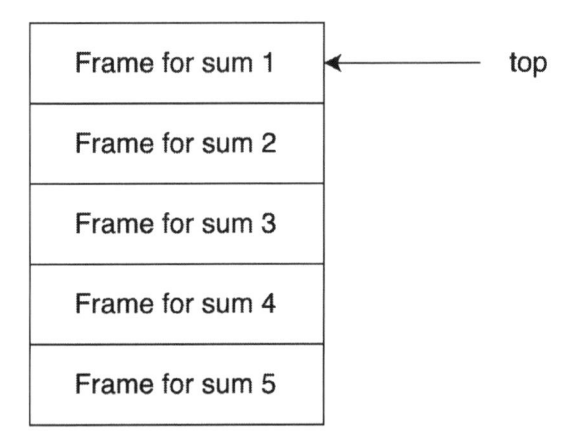

```
┌─────────────────────┐
│   Frame for sum 1   │ ◄────────── top
├─────────────────────┤
│   Frame for sum 2   │
├─────────────────────┤
│   Frame for sum 3   │
├─────────────────────┤
│   Frame for sum 4   │
├─────────────────────┤
│   Frame for sum 5   │
└─────────────────────┘
```

Figure 36: Call stack when executing 'sum 5'

3.4.2 Tail-recursive functions

Let's view the sum function for calculating 1 + 2 + 3 + ... + n again, but differently this time. We maintain a running sum and a counter. Initially, sum is 0 and counter is 1. At each step, sum and counter are updated according to the following rules.

$sum \leftarrow sum + counter$

$counter \leftarrow counter + 1$

The iteration process terminates when counter is greater than n, in which case sum holds the final result.

On the surface, it might seem like we've strayed away from functional programming and slipped back to the imperative paradigm. After all, this is precisely what we did in the imperative Java implementation in the previous section. There, we also maintained a

3 BUILDING ABSTRACTIONS WITH FUNCTIONS

counter and a running sum in a `for` loop. But in this case, we keep the expression-based thinking by formulating the algorithm above as a function.

$$sum(s, c, n) = \begin{cases} s, & \text{for } c > n \\ sum(s + c, c + 1, n), & \text{for } c \leq n \end{cases}$$

Here, the argument s represents the running sum, c represents the counter, and n represents the number of naturals we want to add up.

We can translate this 3-argument function into a recursive function.

```
(* OCaml *)
let rec sum_iter s c n = if c > n then s else
    sum_iter (s + c) (c + 1) n

sum_iter 0 1 3
(* Result: 6 *)
```

Unlike `sum` from the previous section, `sum_iter` does not cause a stack overflow error even in the case of a large argument. For instance, `sum_iter 0 1 1000000` returns a result without any problem.

```
(* OCaml *)
let rec sum_iter s c n = if c > n then s else
    sum_iter (s + c) (c + 1) n

sum_iter 0 1 1000000
(* Result: 500000500000 *)
```

The Art of Functional Programming

3 BUILDING ABSTRACTIONS WITH FUNCTIONS

There is no stack overflow because `sum_iter` is a special kind of recursive function called **tail-recursive** function. It calls itself directly without additional operation. The process of a tail-recursive function, when executed, is very different from that of a non-tail recursive one.

Let's compare the definitions of the two versions `sum` and `sum_iter`, and the processes they evolve.

Non-tail recursive sum

```
(* OCaml *)
let rec sum n = if n <= 0 then 0 else n + sum (n-1)

sum 5
5 + sum 4
5 + (4 + sum 3)
5 + (4 + (3 + sum 2))
5 + (4 + (3 + (2 + sum 1)))
5 + (4 + (3 + (2 + (1 + sum 0))))
5 + (4 + (3 + (2 + (1 + 0))))
5 + (4 + (3 + (2 + 1)))
5 + (4 + (3 + 3))
5 + (4 + 6)
5 + 10
15
```

Tail recursive sum_iter

```
(* OCaml *)
let rec sum_iter s c n = if c > n then s else
    sum_iter (s + c) (c + 1) n

sum 0 1 5
sum_iter 0 1 5
```

The Art of Functional Programming

3 BUILDING ABSTRACTIONS WITH FUNCTIONS

```
6   sum_iter 1 2 5
7   sum_iter 3 3 5
8   sum_iter 6 4 5
9   sum_iter 10 5 5
10  sum_iter 15 6 5
```

In case of `sum`, the chain of deferred calculations is caused by the recursive call being part of an operation `n + sum (n - 1)`. The execution environment uses a call stack to remember where to go back once the deferred calculations are resolved. In case of `sum_iter`, no chain of deferred calculations is built up. As a result, the execution environment does not need to use any call stack to execute a tail-recursive function. This explains why the tail-recursive version does not cause the stack overflow problem.

At this point, we might think that we should always aim to write tail-recursive functions. But that's actually not the case. Looking back, it is clear that the non-recursive version `sum` is much easier to understand than its tail-recursive counterpart. In general, if the recursive function does not operate on too large an input, a naive non-tail recursive solution is usually better.

3.4.3 Tail-recursion optimization

Most functional languages such as OCaml and Haskell support tail-recursion optimization. This means a tail-recursive function is executed without using a call stack. Thanks to this, these languages do not need special-purpose loop constructs, such as **for** and **while**. Recursion alone is enough for implementing loops.

3 BUILDING ABSTRACTIONS WITH FUNCTIONS

On the contrary, most non-functional programming languages do not support tail-recursion optimization. In Java, for instance, the execution of any recursive function, regardless of being tail-recursive or not, pushes frames on a call stack. As a result, any recursive function written in Java causes stack overflow if the number of recursive calls is too high. Because of this, non-functional programming languages introduce special-purpose looping constructs such as `for` and `while` for formulating normal loops that do not cause stack overflow exceptions.

To illustrate, the following OCaml function, `endless`, prints a "Hi recursion" string in an infinite loop in a recursive function.

```
1  (* OCaml *)
2  let rec endless () = print_endline "Hi
       recursion"; endless ()
```

When we run the code, it prints `Hi recursion` in an endless loop but does not throw a stack overflow error.

The following Java function, `endless`, also calls itself recursively to print the string in an endless loop.

```
1   // Java
2   class Test {
3
4     private static void endless() {
5       System.out.println("Hello recursion");
6       endless();
7     }
8
9     public static void main(String[] args) {
10      endless();
11    }
```

3   BUILDING ABSTRACTIONS WITH FUNCTIONS

```
12  }
```

Yet when we run it, we get a stack overflow message. This difference shows that the OCaml compiler implements tail-recursion optimization and compiles the `endless()` function into bytecode that does not rely on a call stack. On the other hand, the Java compiler does not implement tail-recursion optimization. Therefore, it blindly compiles the function into bytecode that uses a call stack to execute the code.

Recursive functions play a vital role in functional programming. Most functional programming languages rely on recursion for formulating loops. As we'll see in the next chapter, many data structures, such as lists or trees, are inherently recursive. Therefore, recursive functions are suitable for defining operations on those structures.

3.5   General Computation Methods as Higher-Order Functions

So far, we've mainly defined functions whose arguments or return values are numbers, boolean values, or strings. But recall that functions are first-class citizens in functional programming languages. Thanks to this, we can easily define a function that accepts other functions as arguments or returns another function as a result. Such a function is called a **higher-order function**. High-order functions are powerful because they enable us to formulate computation patterns that work with different functions.

3.5.1 Summation as a higher-order function

A good way to appreciate the power of functions operating on other functions is to look at summation in mathematics. For instance, mathematicians often study summations, sums of a sequence of numbers, like the sum of all natural numbers from 1 to n:

$1 + 2 + 3 + ... + n$

Or the sum of squares of natural numbers from 1 to n:

$1^2 + 2^2 + 3^2 + ... + n^2$

If we look at these sums of sequences, we can notice that summation can be defined for any function capable of producing the terms for the sum. Of course, mathematicians realized this a long time ago. They invented the summation symbol $\sum$ (read "sigma") to express the sum of elements represented by a function f within an interval, $[m, n]$.

$\sum_{i=m}^{n} f(i) = f(m) + f(m+1) + ... + f(n)$

The following diagram illustrates how the concept of summation is a generalization of more concrete sum concepts:

3 BUILDING ABSTRACTIONS WITH FUNCTIONS

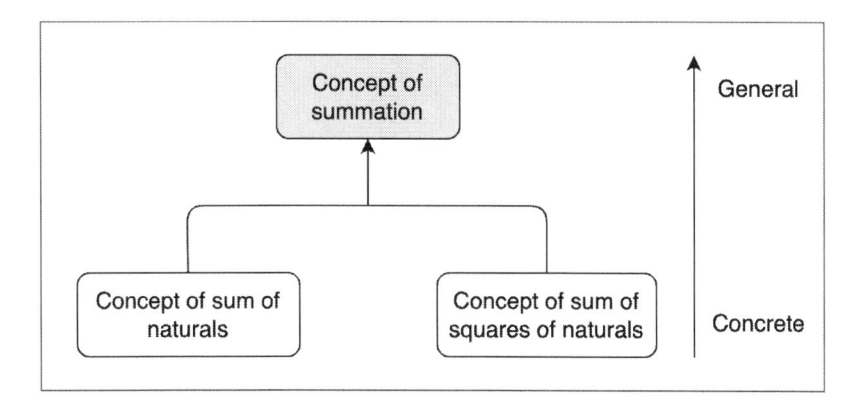

Figure 37: Mathematical summation as generalized concept

What makes $\sum$ so powerful is that it allows mathematicians to think about summation as a concept itself rather than as just the sum of a particular function.

Functional programming readily provides us with a similar power. Let's formulate a higher-order function `sum` in OCaml that behaves similar to the sigma notation $\sum$ above. In particular, it accepts three arguments – a function `term` that maps each index `i` to a term of the sum, the lower index bound `m`, and the upper index bound `n`. For simplicity, we only consider `term` functions that produce terms of type integers.

```
(* OCaml *)
let rec sum term m n = if m > n then 0 else
    term m + sum term (m + 1) n
```

We can easily formulate a function, `sum_integers`, that sums up all integers in a given range with `sum`. In particular, we pass the identity

3 BUILDING ABSTRACTIONS WITH FUNCTIONS

function to sum.

```ocaml
(* OCaml *)
let sum_integers m n = sum (fun i -> i) m n

sum_integers 1 3
(* Result: 6 *)
```

Likewise, the function that calculates the sum of squares of integers within an interval is a particular case of sum.

```ocaml
(* OCaml *)
let sum_integer_squares m n = sum (fun i -> i
     * i) m n

sum_integer_squares 1 3
(* Result: 14 *)
```

What is the difference between the mathematical sigma $\sum$ and our OCaml sum function?

$\sum$ represents a mathematical concept of summation. However, our sum function encapsulates a computation or algorithm that describes how to actually calculate summation. The following figure illustrates this:

3 BUILDING ABSTRACTIONS WITH FUNCTIONS

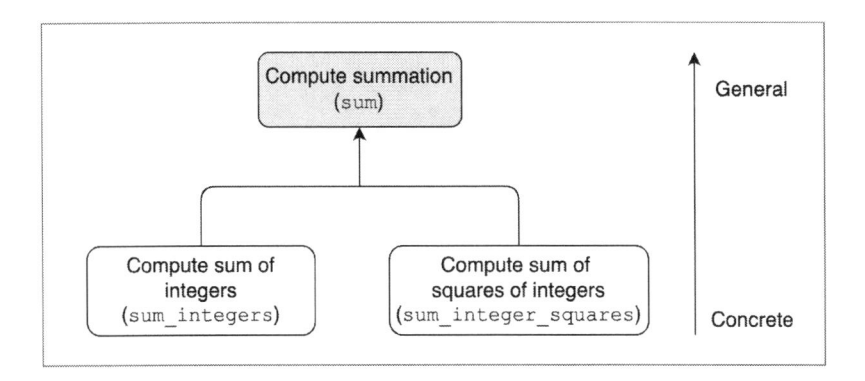

Figure 38: Higher-order function as general method of computation

Although `sum_integers` and `sum_integer_squares` work as expected, their definitions look quite cumbersome. For instance, let's look at `sum_integers` one more time:

```
(* OCaml *)
let sum_integers m n = sum (fun i -> i) m n;;
```

The definition is verbose because the lower and upper bound, m and n, are passed unchanged into sum. Can we get rid of these arguments?

The answer is yes, we can.

```
(* OCaml *)
let sum_integers = sum (fun i -> i)
```

This shorter version works because `sum (fun i -> i)` is a partial function application whose result is a function. We can think of this function as a specialized version of sum where we fix the term function to become (`fun i -> i`). Moreover, since the function accepts two arguments, it precisely defines `sum_integers`.

Similarly, `sum_squares` can be defined more clearly as follows:

```ocaml
(* OCaml *)
let sum_squares = sum (fun i -> i * i)
```

3.5.2 Accumulation as a higher-order function

We can go even further and treat summation as a particular case of accumulation! To illustrate, let's start by observing that mathematicians also think about the products of sequences of numbers. For instance, the factorial of n, denoted by $n!$ is defined as follows:

$n! = 1 \times 2 \times 3 \times ... \times n$

Or the product of squares of natural numbers from 1 to n:

$1^2 \times 2^2 \times 3^2 \times ... \times n^2$

Similar to `sum` discussed previously, we can also define a higher-order function `product` that captures the concept of the product for any function.

```ocaml
(* OCaml *)
let rec product term m n = if m > n then 1
    else term m * product term (m + 1) n;;
```

We use `product` to define a function `product_integers` that calculates the product of integers within an interval.

```ocaml
(* OCaml *)
let product_integers = product (fun x -> x)
```

3 BUILDING ABSTRACTIONS WITH FUNCTIONS

```
3
4  product_integers 1 3
5  (* Result: 6 *)
```

Likewise, we can reuse `product` to formulate a function that calculates the product of the square of integers within an interval.

```
1  (* OCaml *)
2  let product_integer_squares = product (fun x
       -> x * x)
3
4  product_integer_squares 1 3
5  (* Result: 36 *)
```

So far, so good. Yet, `sum` and `product` share a common pattern – both accumulate terms produced by a given function within an interval. This means we can factor out the common pattern into an even more general higher-order function and call it `accumulate`. It takes a binary function, `combiner`, that combines the current term with the previous accumulation. It also accepts an `init` argument that represents an initial value. The last remaining arguments are a `term` function and a range, [m,n].

```
1  (* OCaml *)
2  let rec accumulate combiner init term m n =
3      if m > n then init
4      else combiner (term m) (accumulate
             combiner init term (m + 1) n)
```

Next, we can formulate `sum` and `product` as a particular case of `accumulate`.

```
1  (* OCaml *)
2  let sum = accumulate (+) 0
```

The Art of Functional Programming

3 BUILDING ABSTRACTIONS WITH FUNCTIONS

```
3  let product = accumulate ( * ) 1
4
5  sum (fun x -> x) 1 4
6  (* Result: 10 *)
7  product (fun x -> x) 1 4
8  (* Result: 24 *)
```

3.5.3 Climbing up the abstraction hierarchy

Let's stop and reflect on what we've done so far. We started out with concrete computations, such as the sum of natural numbers, and the sum of squares of natural numbers. Next, we abstracted them into a more general computation summation. However, we soon realized summation is just a particular case of an even more general computation accumulation. This led us to capture accumulation as a higher-order function, `accumulate`. All this was possible because functions are first-class citizens in functional programming languages and hence can accept other functions as arguments.

We can view this remarkable process as climbing up the abstraction hierarchy. The higher we move up, the more general methods of computation we obtain. The following diagram depicts this:

3 BUILDING ABSTRACTIONS WITH FUNCTIONS

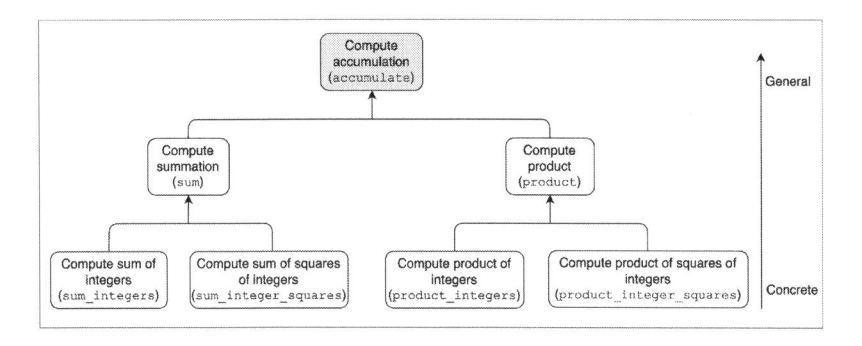

Figure 39: Climbing up the abstraction hierarchy

A general method of computation like `accumulate` has many advantages. First, it avoids code duplication and enables code reusability. In our example, we can reuse `accumulate` to formulate all the functions beneath it in the diagram, such as `sum`, `prod`, `sum_integers`, `prod_integers`, and many others. More importantly, such a general computation method allows us to think about programming on a higher abstraction level. This significantly reduces mental effort when solving programming problems. To see this, let's compare two ways of solving the problem of implementing a function, `sum_integer_cubes n`, that computes $1^3 + 2^3 + ... n^3$.

Low-level thinking

We write a recursive function that returns 0 in case $n < 0$. Otherwise, if the list is `hd :: tl`, we add the cube of `hd` to the recursively calculated result for `tl`.

```
(* OCaml *)
let rec sum_integer_cubes n = if n <= 0 then 0
```

3 BUILDING ABSTRACTIONS WITH FUNCTIONS

```
      else n * n * n + sum_integer_cubes (n -
  1)
```

High-level thinking

We use the `accumulate` computation pattern where the `combiner` is the addition operator +, the `term` function raises an argument to its cube. Moreover, the initial value, `init`, is 0, whereas the range is [1, n].

```
1  (* OCaml *)
2  let sum_integer_cubes = accumulate (+) 0 (fun
       x -> x * x * x) 1
```

Both approaches arrive at a solution for the problem but the thought process is very different. In the first solution, we are concerned about low-level implementation details, such as handling the different recursion cases. In second solution, we pick `accumulate` from a toolbox and focus primarily on how to configure the parameters of `accumulate` to solve the problem. How `accumulate` is implemented is irrelevant to us at this level of abstraction.

3.6 Programming Challenges

3.6.1 Challenge 1: Prime number

Write an OCaml function `is_prime: integer -> bool`, that returns `true` if the input number is a prime number and `false` otherwise.

3   BUILDING ABSTRACTIONS WITH FUNCTIONS

3.6.2 Challenge 2: Naive Fibonacci

The Fibonacci series looks like this: 1 1 2 3 5 8 13 ...

Formally,

```
1  Fibonacci 0 = 0
2  Fibonacci 1 = 1
3  Fibonacci 2 = 1
4  Fibonacci n = Fibonacci (n-1) + Fibonacci (n
       -2) for n > 2
```

Write an OCaml function, `fib: int -> int`, that returns the n-th Fibonacci number where $n \geq 0$.

Examples:

```
1  fib 1 = 1
2  fib 2 = 1
3  fib 3 = 2
4  fib 4 = 3
5  fib 5 = 5
```

3.6.3 Challenge 3: Quick Fibonacci

This is a follow-up to Challenge 2. Try to call `fib 60` with your solution. If it returns the result right away, skip this challenge. However, if `fib 60` seems to run forever, it is likely because your recursive solution performs too many redundant calculations.

Write an improved OCaml version of the previous function, `super_fib: int -> int`, capable of quickly computing a large Fibonacci number like the 60-th one.

3 BUILDING ABSTRACTIONS WITH FUNCTIONS

Examples:

```
1  super_fib 60 = 1548008755920
```

3.6.4 Challenge 4: Apply a function twice

Write an OCaml function called `twice`: `('a -> 'a)-> 'a -> 'a` that applies a unary function, `f`, twice to an argument, `x`. For example, if `inc: int -> int` is the function that increases an input by 1, `twice inc` is a function that increases an input by 2.

Notice that `twice` is a higher-order function because it takes another function as an argument.

Examples:

```
1  twice inc 0 = 2
2  twice inc 1 = 3
3  twice inc 2 = 4
```

Where

```
1  let inc = (+) 1
```

3.6.5 Challenge 5: Compose functions

Suppose `f` and `g` are two unary functions. We define the composition `f` after `g` as the function that maps `x` to `f (g (x))`. Write an OCaml function, `compose: ('a -> 'b)-> ('c -> 'a)-> 'c -> 'b`, that implements the function composition above. For example, suppose `inc` is the function that increases its argument by 1

3 BUILDING ABSTRACTIONS WITH FUNCTIONS

and `double` is a function that multiples an input by 2. The value of (compose `double` inc) 3 is 8 because it increases 3 by 1 and then doubles the result.

Notice that compose is a higher-order because it accepts other functions as arguments.

Examples:

```
1  (compose double inc) 0 = 2
2  (compose double inc) 1 = 4
3  (compose double inc) 2 = 6
```

Where

```
1  let double = ( * ) 2
2  let inc = (+) 1
```

3.6.6 Challenge 6: Filtered accumulation

Recall in this chapter, we defined the following high-order function, accumulate: ('a -> 'b -> 'b)-> 'b -> (int -> 'a) -> int -> int -> 'b, that captures a general computation method for accumulating terms produced by a function within an interval.

```
1  (* OCaml *)
2  let rec accumulate combiner init term m n =
3      if m > n then init
4      else combiner (term m) (accumulate
          combiner init term (m + 1) n);;
```

We can generalize accumulate even further by filtering out

3 BUILDING ABSTRACTIONS WITH FUNCTIONS

terms that satisfy a given predicate. Write an OCaml function `filtered_accumulate`, that takes the same arguments as `accumulate`, along with a predicate p that specifies the filter.

Examples:

```
1  filtered_accumulate (+) 0 (fun x -> x)
       is_prime 1 4 = 5
2  filtered_accumulate (+) 0 (fun x -> x)
       is_prime 2 5 = 10
3  filtered_accumulate (+) 0 (fun x -> x)
       is_prime 3 7 = 15
```

Where `is_prime` checks whether a number is a prime.

3.7 Solutions to Programming Challenges

3.7.1 Challenge 1: Prime number

A number n is prime if we can not find any divisors greater than 1 and less than or equal to the square root of n. A possible implementation in OCaml is shown as below:

```
1  (* OCaml *)
2  let rec is_prime n =
3      if n < 2 then false else if n = 2 then
           true else
4          let rec aux m = if n mod m = 0 then
               false
5                          else if m * m > n then
                              true else aux (m
                              + 1) in aux 2
```

The Art of Functional Programming

3 BUILDING ABSTRACTIONS WITH FUNCTIONS

3.7.2 Challenge 2: Naive Fibonacci

We can translate the Fibonacci definition directly into the following recursive function.

```ocaml
(* OCaml *)
let rec fib n = if n <= 0 then 0 else if n <= 2 then 1 else fib (n - 1) + fib (n - 2)
```

3.7.3 Challenge 3: Quick Fibonacci

At any point, we only need to know two Fibonacci numbers to compute the next one. Based on this insight, we can have the following OCaml implementation:

```ocaml
(* OCaml *)
let super_fib n =
    let rec helper a b m = if m >= n then a
        else helper b (a + b) (m + 1) in
    helper 0 1 0
```

3.7.4 Challenge 4: Apply a function twice

First we apply f to x. Then we apply f to the result of the previous function application.

```ocaml
(* OCaml *)
let twice f x = f (f x)
```

3 BUILDING ABSTRACTIONS WITH FUNCTIONS

3.7.5 Challenge 5: Compose functions

Given an input, x, we first apply g to x. Then we apply f to g x.

```
1  (* OCaml *)
2  let compose f g x = f (g x)
```

3.7.6 Challenge 6: Filtered accumulation

The idea is we only use `combiner` to combine a term if it satisfies the filter. A possible OCaml implementation is shown below:

```
1  let rec filtered_accumulate combiner init term
       p m n =
2    if m > n then init
3    else if p (term m) then combiner (term m)
         (filtered_accumulate combiner init
         term p (m + 1) n)
4    else filtered_accumulate combiner init
         term p (m + 1) n
```

3.8 Quiz on Functions

Let's test your understanding of functions.

3.8.1 Quiz 1

What is the value of the following lambda expression?

$(\lambda x.\, x\, y)(\lambda z.\, z)$

The Art of Functional Programming　　　　　　　　　　　　122

3 BUILDING ABSTRACTIONS WITH FUNCTIONS

Please select all following choices that apply.

Choice A: y

Choice B: z

3.8.2 Quiz 2

What are the key means to create abstractions that functional programming languages provide but imperative programming languages do not?

Please select all following choices that apply.

Choice A: Functions

Choice B: Higher-order functions

3.8.3 Quiz 3

The following code illustrates a function application in OCaml where we apply a constant function to an error argument.

```
(* OCaml *)
fun (x -> "OCaml") (failWith "Something bad
    happen!")
```

The following Haskell code does something similar.

```
-- Haskell
(\x -> "Haskell") (error "Something bad
    happened!")
```

3 BUILDING ABSTRACTIONS WITH FUNCTIONS

What result do we get in OCaml and Haskell?

Please select all following choices that apply.

Choice A:

Result in OCaml:

```
1  Exception: Failure "Something bad happen!".
```

Result in Haskell:

```
1  "Haskell"
```

Choice B:

Result in OCaml:

```
1  "OCaml"
```

Result in Haskell:

```
1  "Haskell"
```

3.8.4 Quiz 4

The OCaml binary operator ^ concatenates two strings. We can wrap it inside parentheses (^) to use it as a normal binary function.

What is the type of (^)?

Please select all following choices that apply.

Choice A: `(string * string)-> string`

Choice B: `string -> string -> string`

3 BUILDING ABSTRACTIONS WITH FUNCTIONS

3.8.5 Quiz 5

The following OCaml function, `endless`, simulates a non-terminating loop using recursion.

```
(* OCaml *)
let rec endless x = endless x
```

What is the result of the following function application in OCaml?

```
(* OCaml *)
(fun x -> 42) (endless 1)
```

Please select all following choices that apply.

Choice A: It never terminates.

Choice B: 42

3.8.6 Quiz 6

What is the result of the following OCaml expression?

```
(* OCaml *)
((>) 10) 9
```

Please select all following choices that apply.

Choice A: The expression is invalid.

Choice B: `true`

Choice B: `false`

The Art of Functional Programming

3 BUILDING ABSTRACTIONS WITH FUNCTIONS

3.8.7 Quiz 7

Given the following OCaml function

```
(* OCaml *)
let judgment f x = if f x then "it's true"
    else "it's false"
```

What is the value of the following OCaml expression?

```
(* OCaml *)
judgment (fun x -> x mod 2 <> 0) 11
```

Please select all following choices that apply.

Choice A: `"it's true"`

Choice B: `"it's false"`

3.8.8 Quiz 8

In this chapter, we defined the following high-order function that captures a general method of accumulation.

```
(* OCaml *)
let rec accumulate combiner init term m n =
        if m > n then init
        else combiner (term m) (accumulate
            combiner init term (m + 1) n)
```

We use `accumulate` to formulate the following function

```
(* OCaml *)
let f n = accumulate (+) 0 (fun x -> let sign
    = if x mod 2 <> 0 then 1 else -1 in sign *
    x) 1 n
```

What does `f` do?

Please select all following choices that apply.

Choice A: It calculates 1 + 2 + 3 + 4 ... + n

Choice B: It calculates 1 - 2 + 3 - 4 + ... n

Choice C: It calculates 1 + 0 + 1 + 0 + ... n

3.9 Answers to Quiz on Functions

3.9.1 Quiz 1

Choice A is correct. The reduction steps looks as follows:

$(\lambda x.\ x\ y)(\lambda z.\ z)$

$(\lambda z.\ z)\ y$

y

3.9.2 Quiz 2

Choice B is correct. Most programming languages allow for defining functions. Yet, what's special about functional programming languages is that they treat functions as first-class citizens. As a result, we can define high-order functions that accept other functions as input or return functions as output. Higher-order functions are vital tools to create abstractions, capturing general methods of computation.

3 BUILDING ABSTRACTIONS WITH FUNCTIONS

3.9.3 Quiz 3

Choice A is correct. Since OCaml is a strict language, the argument is evaluated because the function is applied to it. Conversely, Haskell is a non-strict language and that's why the argument is ignored because it is not used in the function body.

3.9.4 Quiz 4

Choice B is correct. Since -> associates to the right, the type is equivalent to string -> (string -> string). Due to currying, (^) is a function that takes a string as input and returns a function of type string -> string. This resulting function accepts another string and returns the concatenated string.

3.9.5 Quiz 5

Choice A is correct. OCaml has strict semantics. The argument endless 1 is evaluated, although it is not used in the function body.

3.9.6 Quiz 6

Choice B is correct. The binary operator > compares two integers. (>) 10 is a unary function that takes an integer input and returns **true** if 10 is greater than that input and **false** otherwise.

3   BUILDING ABSTRACTIONS WITH FUNCTIONS

3.9.7 Quiz 7

Choice A is correct. The higher-order function `judgment` takes as arguments a function `f` and an argument `x`. If `f x` is **true**, `judgment` equals `it's true`. Otherwise, `judgment` is `"it's false"`.

3.9.8 Quiz 8

Choice B is correct. The `term` function produces elements at the index `i` using the following rules:

- If `i` is an odd number, the term is `i`
- If `i` is an even number, the term is `-i`

4 Compound Data Types

4.1 Group Data Objects into Tuples

Primitive data types such as integers, floats, booleans, and strings are useful but often not sufficient. Yet, when modeling real-world phenomena, we often need to glue together data to form compound data. Consider the example of developing a software package for 2D graphics. To represent, say, a point we could use two separate `float` numbers denoting its x and y coordinate. But this could get messy because we would need to keep track of what x and y coordinates belong to what point. It's much better to glue an x and y coordinate into a compound data object like a pair and treat the point as a single concept.

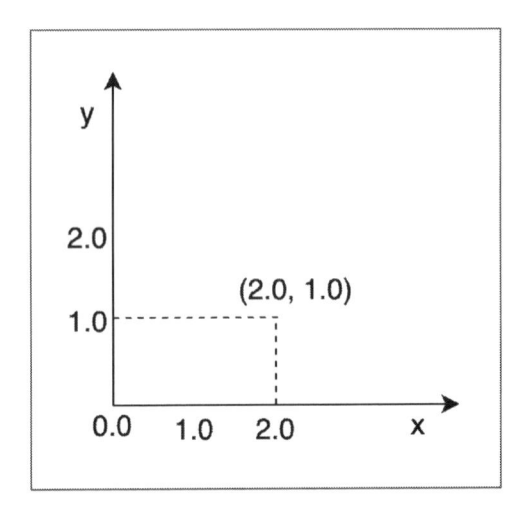

Figure 40: Point on 2D plane

4 COMPOUND DATA TYPES

4.1.1 Construct tuples

OCaml and many other functional programming languages provide the tuples type to group multiple data objects into a single compound data object called a **tuple**. We construct a tuple by placing values into parentheses delimited by commas. For example, we can create a pair, which are tuples of 2 elements.

```
(* OCaml *)
(42, "Hi FP")
```

The order of the elements in a pair is crucial. For instance, ("Hi FP", 42) is an entirely different pair. Moreover, as seen in this example, a pair may contain elements of different types. In our example, the type of (42, "Hi FP") is `int * string`. In general, the pair type, whose first element's type is t1 and the second one is t2, is t1 * t2 (read t1 cross t2).

Tuples have a fixed number of elements and hence are most suited for use cases in which we know the number of elements to be stored in advance. In particular, pair is ideal for representing a 2D point because we need x and y coordinates. We can, for example, define a point with x coordinate = 2.0 and y coordinate = 1.0 as follows:

```
(* OCaml *)
let p = (2., 1.)
```

Other concepts representable as pairs are rational numbers, p/q, and complex numbers, a + bi, where a is the real part and b the imaginary part.

Of course, we can store tuples within tuples. For example, we

4 COMPOUND DATA TYPES

can construct the following pair whose second element is another pair.

```
(* OCaml *)
(1, (2, "FP"))
```

The functional programming language Scheme uses this ability to represent a list as a chain of nested pairs. For instance, the sequence, 1, 2, 3, 4, can be represented as (1, (2, (3, (4, nil)))) in Scheme where `nil` represents an empty list. In OCaml and Haskell, lists are defined using algebraic data types.

Tuples are particularly handy when we want to return more than one value from a function. For instance, when computing an integer division, it can be helpful to obtain the quotient and the remainder at the same time. We can write a `div_mod` function that does integer division of two integers and returns the quotient and the remainder packaged as a pair.

```
(* OCaml *)
let div_mod x y = (x / y, x mod y)

div_mod 5 2
(* Result: (2, 1) *)
```

4.2 Destruct tuples with pattern matching

For tuples to be useful, we need ways to access the elements they contain. Assume we want to define a function `translate_point` that takes a point represented as a pair (x, y) and two translation distances, dx and dy. The function should return a new point whose

4 COMPOUND DATA TYPES

coordinates equal the translated coordinates of the input point.

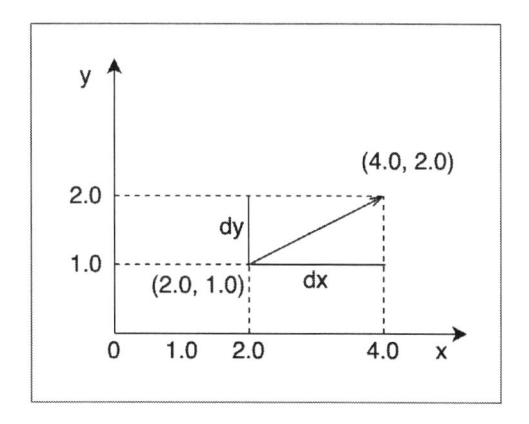

Figure 41: Translating a 2D point

Many functional programming languages, including OCaml and Haskell, provide a powerful mechanism called **pattern matching** to decompose compound data into its components. OCaml supports pattern matching with the match keyword, which we can use to implement translate_point as follows:

```ocaml
(* OCaml *)
let translate_point p dx dy =
    match p with
    | (x, y) -> (x +. dx, y +. dy)

translate_point (2., 1.) 2. 1.
(* Result: (4., 2.) *)
```

Note that match deconstructs an input point p into the (x, y) value and binds the coordinate values to x and y. This allows us to access the x and y coordinates in our implementation.

4 COMPOUND DATA TYPES

Consider another example of implementing a `distance_point` function that calculates the distance between two points. We know that the distance of two points (x_1, y_1) and (x_2, y_2) is calculated by the formula, $\sqrt{(x_1 - x_2)^2 + (y_1 - y_2)^2}$

In OCaml, we can implement `distance_point` with two pattern matches.

```
(* OCaml *)
let distance_point p1 p2 =
    match p1 with
    | (x1, y1) -> match p2 with
                  | (x2, y2) -> sqrt ((x1 -. x2) ** 2. +. (y1 -. y2) ** 2.);;

distance_point (2., 1.) (4., 2.)
(* Result: 2.236 *)
```

The two nested `match` patterns are a bit cumbersome and difficult to read. Fortunately, OCaml allows us to perform two pattern matches at once.

```
(* OCaml *)
let distance_point p1 p2 =
    match p1, p2 with
    | (x1, y1), (x2, y2) -> sqrt ((x1 -. x2) ** 2. +. (y1 -. y2) ** 2.)
```

Pattern matching is so useful that OCaml provides syntactic sugar for using it in a `let` binding or `fun` definition. In particular, we can define `distance_point` very succinctly as follows:

```
(* OCaml *)
let distance_point (x1, y1) (x2, y2) = sqrt ((
```

```
    x1 -. x2) ** 2. +. (y1 -. y2) ** 2.)
```

We could improve the `translate_point` function discussed earlier by pattern matching the point argument directly in the argument.

```
1  (* OCaml *)
2  let translate_point (x, y) dx dy = (x +. dx, y
       +. dy)
```

4.2.1 Data is immutable in functional programming

One key aspect when programming in the functional paradigm is that data is immutable. That means once a data object is constructed, we cannot change it. This contrasts with mutable data in the imperative programming paradigm where the state of the data can be changed after the data is created.

OCaml tuples are immutable. We can see this implication in the `translate_point` function from the previous section.

```
1  (* OCaml *)
2  let translate_point (x, y) dx dy = (dx +. x,
       dy +. y)
```

When we translate a point, we do not call a method or something like that to update its coordinates to new values. In fact, we can't do that because the `(x, y)` pair is immutable and can't be modified. Instead, we construct an entirely new point that contains the coordinates calculated from the old point.

4 COMPOUND DATA TYPES

Immutable data has a lot of advantages. First, it makes understanding programs easier. When we look at an immutable data object, we know immediately what it carries. This is not the case with mutable data because the state of mutable data might change over time. To derive the current values of mutable data, we have to trace back its entire change history. Another advantage of immutable data is thread safety.

Immutable data leads to a typical programming style where a function creates entirely new data from input data. This might feel awkward at first, but once we get used to immutable data, we can understand all its benefits and how pleasant it is to work with.

4.3 Store Sequences of Data with Lists

When modeling real-world phenomena, we often need to model an ordered sequence of data of the same type, such as a sequence of integers `1, 2, 3` or of strings `"Joe"; "Bob"; "Lena"`. If a 2D point is represented as a pair of x and y coordinates, we might want to model a sequence of 2D points `(1.0, 1.0); (2.0, 1.0); (3.0, 0.0)`. Most functional programming languages, including OCaml, provide the list data structure for representing these kinds of data.

4.3.1 Construct and destruct lists

There are two data constructors to construct a list. The first constructor, `[]` (read as nil), creates an empty list. An empty list con-

4 COMPOUND DATA TYPES

tains no elements.

The second data constructor, :: (read as cons) takes two arguments — the first element of the list and another list. For instance, we can use :: to create a list containing the integer 2 by consing 2 to the empty list [].

```
1  (* OCaml *)
2  2::[]
```

The list containing 1 and 2 in that order is constructed by consing 1 onto the list, 2::[].

```
1  (* OCaml *)
2  1::(2::[])
```

For constructing lists, OCaml provides syntactic sugar that looks more familiar.

```
1  (* OCaml *)
2  [1; 2; 3]
```

When we write [1; 2; 3], OCaml internally desugars — or translates — the expression into (1::(2::(3::[]))).

The way we use :: to construct a list by consing an element to the beginning of an existing list reveals that the list in OCaml is a singly linked list. The following diagram shows how the [1; 2; 3] list is represented as a singly linked list whereby the empty list, [], signals the end of the list.

4 COMPOUND DATA TYPES

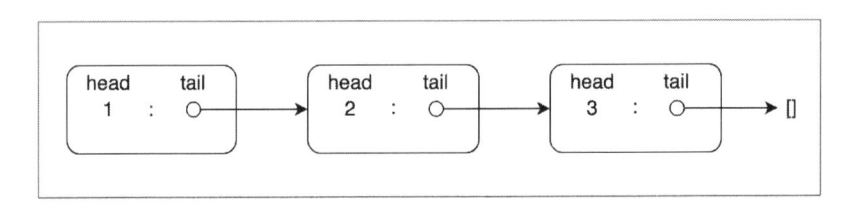

Figure 42: Singly-linked list based OCaml lists

Let's apply what we've learned to write an OCaml function, `enumerate_integers`, that takes two arguments – a and b – and enumerates a list of integers within the interval [a, b].

```
(* OCaml *)
let rec enumerate_integers a b =
    if a > b then [] else a ::
        enumerate_integers (a + 1) b

enumerate_integers 1 10
(* Result: [1; 2; 3; 4; 5; 6; 7; 8; 9; 10] *)
```

The key idea here is, starting from a, we keep consing a new number onto the list until we reach b.

We rely on pattern matching to destruct a list into its components when we need to access the elements of the list. Since there are two data constructors for lists, pattern matching for lists typically looks as follows:

```
(* OCaml *)
match l with
| [] ->
| hd :: tl ->
```

That means either the list is an empty list, [], or a non-empty list of

4 COMPOUND DATA TYPES

the shape `hd :: tl`. In the latter case, `hd` holds the head, or the first element of the list, whereas `tl` is the tail, or the remaining list containing all but the first element.

Let's use pattern matching to implement two functions, `hd` and `tl`, which extract a list's head and tail. Since an empty list has neither head nor tail, we throw an exception with `failwith` in that case.

```
(* OCaml *)
let hd l = match l with
           | [] -> failwith "Empty list"
           | x :: _ -> x


let tl l = match l with
           | [] -> failwith "Empty list"
           | _ :: xs -> xs

hd [1; 2; 3]
(* Result: 1 *)
tl [1; 2; 3]
(* Result: [2; 3] *)
```

In fact, the OCaml `List` module already contains these two functions. We can use them via `List.hd` and `List.tl`.

4.3.2 List operations

When we pattern match a list, we can only access its head element. To access elements further down the list, we need to successively pattern match the tail, then the tail's tail, and so on and so forth. This is a common technique when working with lists. For example, let's write a `nth` function that accepts an `n` index and a list and re-

4 COMPOUND DATA TYPES

turns the `n-th` element of the list. We assume that the list elements are numbered, beginning with 0.

```
(* OCaml *)
let rec nth l n = if n <= 0 then List.hd l
    else nth (List.tl l) (n-1)

nth [1; 2; 3] 1
(* Result: 2 *)
```

Here, we keep examining the tail part of the list recursively until we find the element. OCaml provides this function in the `List` module. Replace `nth [1; 2; 3] 1` by `List.nth [1; 2; 3] 1` to see that they return the same result.

When implementing recursive functions on lists, we can rely on the empty list `[]` as a marker for the base case of the recursion. To illustrate, let's implement a `length` function that returns the length of a list.

```
(* OCaml *)
let rec length l = match l with
                   | [] -> 0
                   | hd :: tl -> 1 + length tl

length [1; 2; 3]
(* Result: 3 *)
```

Notice that the recursion stops when we reach the empty list `[]`. This function is also provided in OCaml's `List` module. Try to use `List.length` in the code above to see how its behavior is similar to our `length` function.

Another common pattern is to pattern match a list consecutively

4 COMPOUND DATA TYPES

while building up another list via the list constructor ::, as with the append function for concatenating two lists.

```
(* OCaml *)
let rec append l1 l2 = match l1 with
                       | [] -> l2
                       | x :: xs -> x :: append xs l2
append [1; 2; 3] [4; 5; 6]
```

In fact, OCaml built-operator @ behaves the exact same way as append. Try to replace append [1; 2; 3] [4; 5; 6] with [1; 2; 3] @ [4; 5; 6] see what the result is.

4.3.3 Immutable list vs. array

OCaml lists are immutable. Once a list is constructed, we cannot modify it. When we append a new element to the beginning of an existing list using the constructor ::, a new list is created from the old list.

If you're new to functional programming, it might feel awkward to work with lists. To illustrate, assume we want to change the first element of the l = [1; 2; 3] list above to 4 so that the resulting list is [4; 2; 3]. Due to immutability, we can not modify it. Instead, we have to construct a new list where the first element is 4 and the remaining elements are the tail of the original list.

```
(* OCaml *)
4 :: (List.tl l)
```

Why don't we just use arrays like C or Java? They allow random

4 COMPOUND DATA TYPES

access, which is a very convenient feature. Indeed, we can simply change the first element of a Java array directly. The following Java code illustrates this:

```
1  // Java
2  int[] a = {1, 2, 3};
3  a[0] = 4;
4  // a becomes {4, 2, 3}
```

Here, a[0] changes the first element to 4.

On the surface, Java arrays seem more comfortable to use. A Java array resembles a collection of memory cells that can be accessed and updated via an index. Yet a Java array's flexibility is also its weakness. Java arrays are mutable, which means their elements can be freely modified even after the arrays have been created. This can make it very hard to understand programs containing arrays in some cases. As an extreme example, consider the following Java code snippet:

```
1  // Java
2  int[] a = {1, 2, 3};
3  int[] b = a;
4  b[0] = 42;
5  // a becomes {42, 2, 3}
```

Although we do not declare any statement to modify a, its value is changed to [42, 2, 3] because b refers to it and is used to change its first element. These types of programs can be difficult to debug.

In contrast, lists in OCaml and other functional programming languages are immutable. They do not suffer from those problems as

4 COMPOUND DATA TYPES

arrays. Once a list is constructed, its elements remain the same. If an OCaml function needs to return a list, it creates an entirely new list.

Shifting from arrays to immutable lists poses a challenge to many people new to functional programming. This is totally understandable. Arrays are among the most common data structures in mainstream programming languages.

To get used to the functional way of working with lists, let's implement the `reverse` function in functional style with OCaml, as well as in the imperative style with Java.

Reverse a list in functional style with OCaml

```
1  (* OCaml *)
2  let rec reverse l = match l with
3                     | [] -> l
4                     | hd :: tl -> (reverse tl
                      ) @ [hd];;
```

Reverse an array in imperative style with Java

```
1  void reverse(int[] a) {
2    for (int i = 0; i < a.length / 2; i++) {
3      int temp = a[i];
4      a[i] = a[a.length - 1 - i];
5      a[a.length - 1 - i] = temp;
6    }
7  }
```

In the functional style, we construct a new list with the same elements as the input, only in the reserve order. In the imperative Java version, we change the input array directly via in-place updates.

The functional style version is much easier to understand and closer to our intuition of a mathematical function. The function produces a new expression from an input expression. Moreover, it always produces the same output for the same input.

4.3.4 Lists are generic containers

The list data structure contains other elements and exemplifies what is called a container. Lists are generic containers in the sense that they can hold elements of any type. We have seen lists of integers, strings, or pairs. However, a list might well contain functions or even other lists as elements. In fact, as we'll see in the next section, we can easily define a custom type and use a list to store a sequence of data of that type.

OCaml defines the list type as `'a list`. Here, `'a` (or alpha) is a type variable and stands for any type. For instance, `int list` is a list of integers, `string list` is a list of strings, and `(float * float) list` is a list of pairs of floats.

One big advantage of list being a generic container is that we can define generic functions that work on lists regardless of their element types. This style of programming is known as generic programming. The `length` function defined in the previous section is an example of that.

```
(* OCaml *)
let rec length l = match l with
                   | [] -> 0
                   | hd :: tl -> 1 + length tl
```

4 COMPOUND DATA TYPES

The type of `length` is `'a list -> int` indicates that it works for any list, whether it's a list of integers, a list of strings, or a list of elements of a custom type. This is a huge deal because writing a separate length function for every concrete list would be extremely tedious.

Similarly, the OCaml operator `@`: `'a list -> 'a list -> 'a list` is also a generic function as it can append two lists of any type.

4.4 Declare User-defined Types with Algebraic Data Types

There are two main ways to construct compound datatypes:

- Combination: We define a complex datatype by combining other types. For instance, the pair type `int * string` consists of all combinations whose first component is an integer and a string. This kind of type is also called a product type because it resembles the Catesian product.
- Alternation: We define a type as a set of alternatives. For example, the list data type is represented by two alternatives. One alternative is `[]`, the other is a pair —a combination itself— containing the head and the tail. A type defined this way is also known as sum type. This type is the sum of all alternatives.

Algebraic data types provide a universal mechanism to define structured data by blending the power of both combination and alternation. The term algebraic comes from the properties that an algebraic datatype is created from sum and product.

4.4.1 Example – modeling geometric shapes

Suppose we want to model geometric shapes. For the sake of simplicity, we consider two kinds of shapes, circle and rectangle. Moreover, a circle is associated with a radius, while a rectangle has a width and length. We can represent shape as an algebraic data type as follows.

```
1  (* OCaml *)
2  type shape =   Circle of float
3                | Rectangle of float * float
```

The two kinds of shapes are represented by two different data constructors, `Circle` and `Rectangle` separated by the bar symbol |. Furthermore, the `Circle` constructor carries the circle's radius as a float, whereas `Rectangle` requires two floats denoting the rectangle's width and height.

With this definition, we can use the constructors to create shape values. For example, we can create several shapes and store them in a list.

```
1  (* OCaml *)
2  [Circle 2.; Circle 3.; Rectangle (1., 2.)]
```

Moreover, an algebraic data type can be defined in terms of itself, making it ideal for modeling a recursive structure. For instance, we may add a new `ComplexShape` constructor that represents a shape

4 COMPOUND DATA TYPES

composed of other shapes.

```ocaml
(* OCaml *)
type shape = Circle of float
           | Rectangle of float * float
           | ComplexShape of shape list
```

This algebraic datatype is recursive because the ComplexShape constructor refers to shape in its definition.

For example, with this definition, we can define a complex shape consisting of three other shapes – circle, rectangle, and another complex shape.

```ocaml
(* OCaml *)
ComplexShape [Circle 1.; Rectangle (2., 3.);
    ComplexShape [Circle 4.; Circle 5.]]
```

Like tuples and lists, we use pattern matching to deconstruct a value of an algebraic datatype into its various cases. For instance, let's write a function, area: shape -> float, to calculate the area of a shape.

```ocaml
(* OCaml *)
let rec area s =
  match s with
  | Circle r -> 3.14 *. r *. r
  | Rectangle (w, h) -> w *. h
  | ComplexShape l -> match l with
                      | [] -> 0.
                      | hd :: tl -> area hd +.
                          area (ComplexShape
                          tl)

area (ComplexShape [Circle 1.; Rectangle (2.,
    3.); ComplexShape [Circle 4.]])
```

4 COMPOUND DATA TYPES

```
11  (* Result: 59.38 *)
```

The `area` function matches three patterns corresponding to shape three data constructors. In the first two patterns, `Circle` and `Rectangle`, we use well-known formulas to calculate the area of a circle and rectangle respectively. The last pattern match for `ComplexShape` calculates a complex shape by recursively summing up the areas of the child shapes. For simplicity, we assume that the child shapes of a complex shape do not overlap.

As you can see, the power of algebraic datatypes stems from the ability to define a type as a set of constructors. Each constructor might carry zero, one, or multiple pieces of data. Moreover, an algebraic data type can be defined in terms of itself, making it easy to define recursive structures.

4.4.2 Parameterized algebraic datatypes

Algebraic datatypes have another powerful feature – they can be parameterized over other types. This allows us to define generic datatypes, much like a list that contains elements of any type.

Consider the problem of modeling a binary tree, which is either a leaf with no fields or a node containing a left tree, the data, and a right tree. We can translate this definition directly into an algebraic datatype.

```
1  (* OCaml *)
2  type 'a bin_tree =
3    | Leaf
4    | Node of 'a bin_tree * 'a * 'a bin_tree
```

4 COMPOUND DATA TYPES

By parameterizing `bin_tree` over a type variable `'a`, we effectively define `bin_tree` as a generic container that can hold elements of any type.

The following diagram shows an example of a binary tree with 4 nodes of integers and how they're represented as `bin_tree`.

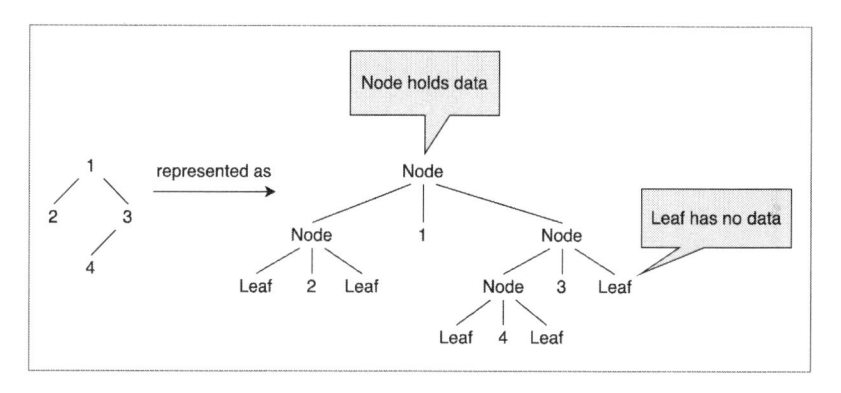

Figure 43: A binary tree represented as algebraic data type

The example tree in the diagram above is represented by the following expression:

```
(* OCaml *)
(Node (Node (Leaf, 2, Leaf), 1, Node (Node (
    Leaf, 4, Leaf), 3, Leaf)))
```

As with any generic datatype, we can write generic functions that work for binary trees of any type. For example, we can write a `size` function to return the size of a binary tree – that is, the number of its nodes.

```
(* OCaml *)
```

4   COMPOUND DATA TYPES

```
2  let rec size t =
3    match t with
4    | Leaf -> 0
5    | Node (l, _, r) -> size l + 1 + size r;;
6
7  size (Node (Node (Leaf, 2, Leaf), 1, Node (
       Node (Leaf, 4, Leaf), 3, Leaf)))
8  (* Result: 4 *)
```

We could modify `size` to define a `sum_tree` function that calculates the sum of all nodes in a tree of integers.

```
1  (* OCaml *)
2  let rec sum_tree t =
3    match t with
4    | Leaf -> 0
5    | Node (l, x, r) -> sum_tree l + x +
       sum_tree r
6
7  sum_tree (Node (Node (Leaf, 2, Leaf), 1, Node
       (Node (Leaf, 4, Leaf), 3, Leaf)))
8  (* Result: 10 *)
```

We can parameterize an algebraic datatype over multiple type variables. For instance, a popular data structure in functional programming languages is `Either`, which captures values with two possibilities. The typical way to define `Either` is as an algebraic datatype parameterized over two type variables. In OCaml, we use the below syntax to define it:

```
1  (* OCaml *)
2  type ('a, 'b) either = Left of 'a | Right of '
       b
```

Note that we name the type `either` because OCaml types must be

The Art of Functional Programming   150

4 COMPOUND DATA TYPES

in lowercase. In Haskell, it is called `Either` (uppercase).

As a convention, `Right of 'b` holds the correct (right) value while `Left of 'a` represents an error value. We can use `either` as the return type of a `safe_div` function that divides a dividend a by a divisor b. If the divisor is not 0, the function returns the division result. Otherwise, it returns a string, `Division by zero`.

```
1  (* OCaml *)
2  let safe_div a b = if b <> 0 then Right (a / b
      ) else Left "Division by zero"
3
4  safe_div 5 2
5  (* Result: 2 *)
6  safe_div 5 0
7  (* Result: Left "Division by zero" *)
```

4.4.3 Algebraic datatypes as a foundation for built-in types

Algebraic datatypes are so powerful that OCaml uses them to define several important built-in datatypes.

Bool

```
1  type bool = True | False
```

The two data constructors, `True` and `False`, are written in uppercase. However, we have to use them in lowercase, **true** and **false**.

List

Internally, OCaml defines a list as an algebraic datatype.

4 COMPOUND DATA TYPES

```ocaml
(* OCaml *)
type 'a list = [] | :: of 'a * 'list;;
```

Notice that we couldn't define this type ourselves because :: is not a valid name for a data constructor in OCaml. However, we might name the two data constructors, `Nil` and `Cons`, to define a list type ourselves.

```ocaml
(* OCaml *)
type 'a mylist = Nil | Cons of 'a * 'a mylist
```

Option type

Functional programming languages typically introduce a datatype called an `option` type. It models two possible outcomes—no value exists, or some value exists. Options can be perfectly modeled as an algebraic datatype with two constructors. In particular, OCaml's built-in `option` type is defined using the command below:

```ocaml
(* OCaml *)
type 'a option = None | Some 'a
```

The `option` type is helpful when we define a function that might not return a meaningful result in some cases. For instance, suppose we want to write a function, `list_max`, that produces the maximum value in a list.

```ocaml
(* OCaml *)
let rec list_max l =
  match l with
  | [] -> What should we do?
  | hd :: tl -> max hd (list_max tl)
```

The Art of Functional Programming

4 COMPOUND DATA TYPES

Here, the OCaml built-in function `max` returns the maximum of two input arguments.

What should we return in case of an empty list `[]`? Since no maximum value exists, the most meaningful value we can return is `None`. That means we can define `list_max` using `option`, as shown below:

```ocaml
(* OCaml *)
let rec list_max l =
  match l with
  | [] -> None
  | hd :: tl -> match list_max tl with
                | None -> Some hd
                | Some m -> Some (max hd m)

list_max [1; 2; 3]
(* Result: Some 3 *)
list_max []
(* Result: None *)
```

The `option` type is quite similar to the `either` type defined in the previous section. The main difference is `either` allows us to provide extra information in both cases, `Left` and `Right`. In contrast, `option` does not require any data in the case of `None`.

4.4.4 Algebraic datatypes vs. classes

If you are used to object-oriented programming, you might be asking, "Are algebraic data types the same as classes?" Indeed, we might model geometric shapes by defining a base class `Shape`. Circles, rectangles, and complex shapes are represented by classes

4 COMPOUND DATA TYPES

`Circle`, `Rectangle` and `ComplexShape`, all inherited from `Shape`.

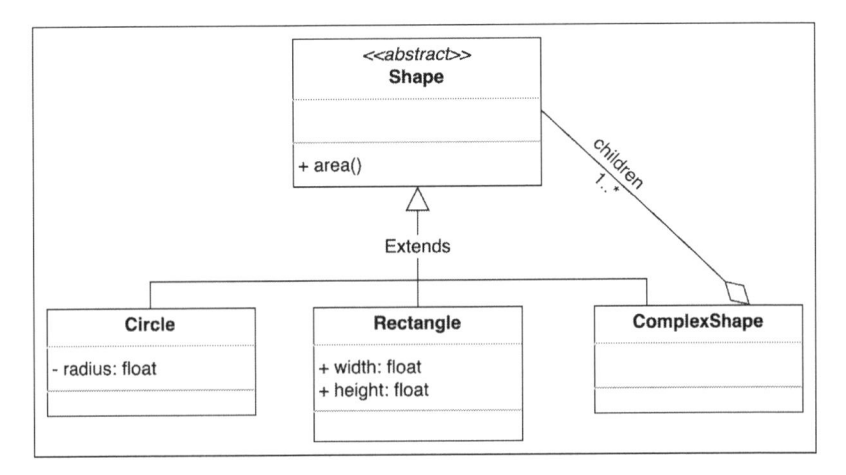

Figure 44: Modeling geometric shapes with classes and inheritance

Despite their similar appearance, the use cases for classes differ from algebraic datatypes significantly. In particular, classes together with inheritance make it easy to extend the set of representations for the type. However, adding a new operation to the class type is difficult. With algebraic datatypes and pattern matching, the situation is reversed. While it is effortless to extend the set of operations on an algebraic dat type, it is difficult to add a representation to an algebraic datatype.

Let's use the example of shapes to illustrate this further. Consider a case where we have to model shapes as a hierarchy of classes. What if we need to handle a new kind of shape, triangles? We can easily accomplish this with classes. We simply add a new subclass, `Triangle`, inherited from `Shape`.

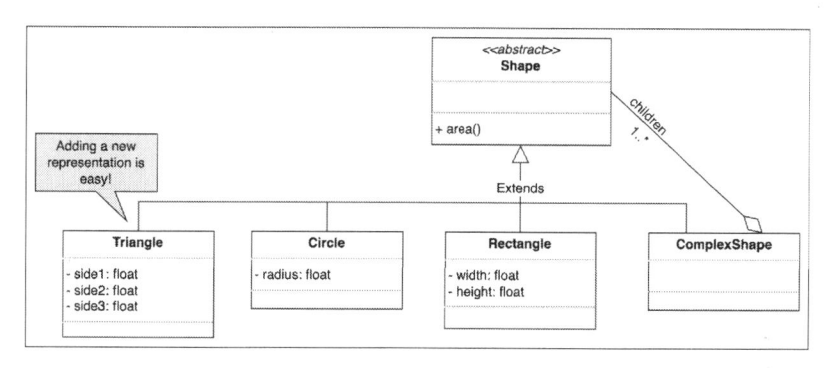

Figure 45: Add a new class to class hierarchy

When we want to add a new data representation via `Triangle`, we don't need to make any changes the `shape` base class or the subclasses – `Circle`, `Rectangle`, and `ComplexShape`.

Unfortunately, modeling shapes as a hierarchy of classes has a big limitation. Adding a new operation, such as `perimeter`, to calculate the shape's perimeter is difficult. We need to add a method declaration to the `Shape` base class and add a method definition to every existing subclass. However, this is expensive because the subclasses might be distributed everywhere.

When we model shapes as an algebraic datatype, what does the situation look like? It is the opposite. We can add a new operation over the algebraic datatype, such as `perimeter: shape -> **float**` without any problem. The implementation is straightforward – we rely on pattern matching to calculate the perimeter of every kind

4 COMPOUND DATA TYPES

of shape. For simplicity, we assume the child shapes of a complex one do not overlap. The perimeter of a complex shape is supposed to equal the total of the child shapes.

```
(* OCaml *)
let rec perimeter s =
  match s with
  | Circle r -> 2. *. Float.pi *. r
  | Rectangle (w, h) -> 2. *. (w +. h)
  | ComplexShape l -> match l with
                      | [] -> 0.
                      | hd :: tl -> perimeter
                        hd +. perimeter (
                        ComplexShape tl)
```

Note that when we add this operation, it does not affect the functionality of existing operations, such as `area`.

However, adding a new data representation is problematic. Suppose we extend `shape` with a new data constructor `Triangle`.

```
(* OCaml *)
type shape = Circle of float
           | Rectangle of float * float
           | Triangle of float * float * float
           | ComplexShape of shape list
```

This change forces us to modify all operations over `shape` because they need to match a new pattern for `Triangle`. This is expensive since operations can be located in different places.

The following diagram visualizes the illustrated difference between classes and inheritance, and algebraic datatypes and pattern matching:

4   COMPOUND DATA TYPES

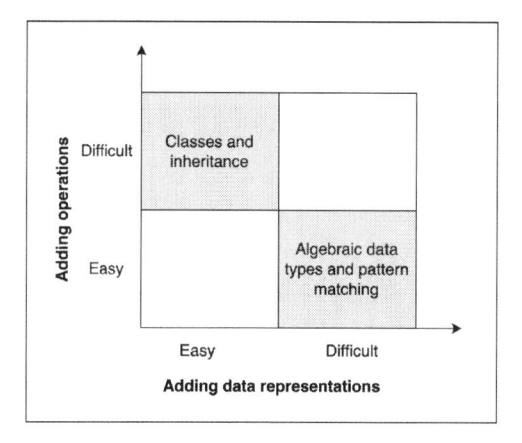

Figure 46: Comparing classes and inheritance with algebraic datatypes and pattern matching

This shows that both – classes and inheritance, as well as algebraic datatypes and pattern matching – have their strengths and weaknesses in modeling data. This is one of the reasons that many programming languages, OCaml included, decide to support both.

This shows that both – classes and inheritance, as well as algebraic datatypes and pattern matching – have their strengths and weaknesses in modeling data. This is one of the reasons that many programming languages, OCaml included, decide to support both.

This naturally leads to the question, "Is there any data abstraction that makes it easy to add new data representations and new operations while retaining static type safety?" That question is precisely what the computer scientist Philip Wadler termed the expression problem. As of today, despite many proposed solutions, it is still not definitively solved. Until there is a definite solution to that problem,

4 COMPOUND DATA TYPES

what we can do is remember our rules of thumb – use classes and inheritance to conveniently add data representations, and use algebraic datatypes and pattern matching to extend operations without compiling the code.

4.5 Programming Challenges

Let's solve coding challenges to practice compound datatypes.

4.5.1 Challenge 1: Find the longest string in a string list

Write an OCaml function, `longest_string: string list -> string option`, to find the longest string in a list of strings.

Examples:

```
(* OCaml *)
longest_string [] = None
longest_string ["a"; "abc"; "ab"] = Some "abc"
```

Hint: You can use OCaml's `String.length` function to compute the length of a string.

4.5.2 Challenge 2: Concatenate strings

Write an OCaml function, `concat: string -> string list -> string`, to add a string `s` and a list of string `l`, and then concatenate all the strings in the list delimited by `s`.

Examples:

4 COMPOUND DATA TYPES

```
(* OCaml *)
concat "," [] = ""
concat "," ["a"] = "a"
concat "," ["a"; "b"] = "a,b"
concat "--" ["a"; "b"; "c"] = "a--b--c"
```

4.5.3 Challenge 3: Find the height of a binary tree

The following algebraic datatype represents a binary tree in this chapter.

```
(* OCaml *)
type 'a bin_tree =
  | Leaf
  | Node of 'a bin_tree * 'a * 'a bin_tree
```

Write an OCaml function, `height: 'a bin_tree -> int`, to return the height of a binary tree. The height of the binary tree is the longest path from the root node to any leaf in the tree.

Examples:

```
(* OCaml *)
height Leaf = 0
height (Node (Node (Leaf, 2, Leaf), 1, Node (
    Node (Leaf, 4, Leaf), 3, Leaf))) = 3
```

4.5.4 Challenge 4: Find the predecessor of natural number

We can define an algebraic datatype to represent natural numbers.

4 COMPOUND DATA TYPES

Example:

```ocaml
(* OCaml *)
type nat = Zero | Succ of nat
```

Following this definition, `Zero` represents 0, `Succ Zero` represents 1, `Succ (Succ Zero)` represents 2, `Succ (Succ (Succ Zero))` represents 3, and so on.

Write an OCaml function, `pred: nat -> nat option`, that takes n of type `nat` as input and returns its predecessor. Beware that `pred Zero` does not exist. If the implementation returns `pred Zero = Zero`, it may need correction.

Examples:

```ocaml
(* OCaml *)
pred Zero = None
pred (Succ Zero) = Some Zero
pred (Succ (Succ Zero)) = Some (Succ Zero)
```

4.5.5 Challenge 5: Add two natural numbers

This is a follow-up to Challenge 4 in which we defined the following algebraic datatype to represent natural numbers.

Example:

```ocaml
(* OCaml *)
type nat = Zero | Succ of nat
```

Write an OCaml function, `add: nat -> nat`, to add two numbers of `nat` type and return the result of the same type.

4 COMPOUND DATA TYPES

Examples:

```
(* OCaml *)
add Zero Zero = Zero
add Zero (Succ Zero) = Succ Zero
add (Succ Zero) (Succ Zero) = Succ (Succ Zero)
```

4.6 Solutions to Programming Challenges

4.6.1 Challenge 1: Find the longest string in a string list

We write a recursive function that pattern matches two list constructors. Also, we need to pattern match the call of `longest_string` to the tail of the list.

```
(* OCaml *)
let rec longest_string l =
  match l with
  | [] -> None
  | hd :: tl ->
      let s = longest_string tl in
      match s with
      | None -> Some hd
      | Some x -> if String.length hd >
        String.length x then Some hd else
        Some x
```

4.6.2 Challenge 2: Concatenate strings

We write a recursive function that pattern matches three possible cases: empty list [], list of a single element, and list of two or more elements.

4 COMPOUND DATA TYPES

```
(* OCaml *)
let rec concat s l =
  match l with
  | [] -> ""
  | hd :: [] -> hd
  | hd :: tl -> hd ^ s ^ (concat s tl);;
```

4.6.3 Challenge 3: Find the height of a binary tree

We pattern match a tree with two cases. If the tree is Leaf, the height is 0. Otherwise, if the tree is a Node, the height is one plus the max height of the left and right subtree.

```
(* OCaml *)
let rec height t =
  match t with
  | Leaf -> 0
  | Node (l, _, r) -> 1 + max (height l) (
    height r)
```

4.6.4 Challenge 4: Find the predecessor of natural number

We pattern match two constructors, Zero and Succ. In case of Zero, there is predecessor. In case of Succ x, the predecessor is x.

```
(* OCaml *)
let pred n = match n with
             | Zero -> None
             | Succ x -> Some x
```

The Art of Functional Programming

4 COMPOUND DATA TYPES

4.6.5 Challenge 5: Add two natural numbers

To add two naturals m and n, we keep decreasing m while increasing n, until m becomes Zero.

```
(* OCaml *)
let rec add n m = match m with
                  | Zero -> n
                  | Succ x -> add (Succ n) x
```

4.7 Quiz on Compound Datatypes

Let's test your understanding of compound datatypes.

4.7.1 Quiz 1

How many elements of the triple (3-tuple) type, string * int * bool, can we have?

Please select all following choices that apply.

Choice A: 1 element

Choice B: An infinite number of elements

4.7.2 Quiz 2

How many elements of the following algebraic datatype can we have?

4   COMPOUND DATA TYPES

```ocaml
(* OCaml *)
type mytype = BoolVal of bool | Constant
```

Please select all following choices that apply.

Choice A: 3 elements

Choice B: Infinitely many elements

4.7.3 Quiz 3

What does the following function do?

```ocaml
(* OCaml *)
let safe_hd l = match l with
                | [] -> None
                | hd :: tl -> Some hd
```

Please select all following choices that apply.

Choice A: If the list is not empty, it returns the head of the list wrapped inside Some. If the list is empty, it returns None.

Choice B: If the list is not empty, it returns the head of the list. If the list is empty, it throws an exception.

4.7.4 Quiz 4

Given the following list in OCaml:

```ocaml
(* OCaml *)
let l = ["Joe"; "Adam"; "Anna"]
```

4 COMPOUND DATA TYPES

What does the following expression do?

```
(* OCaml *)
l[0] = "John"
```

Please select all following choices that apply.

Choice A: It updates the first element of l to "John" resulting in ["John"; "Adam"; "Anna"].

Choice B: It's not a valid OCaml expression.

4.7.5 Quiz 5

The following algebraic data type represents geometric shapes:

```
(* OCaml *)
type shape =  Circle of float
            | Rectangle of float * float
            | ComplexShape of shape list
```

We decide to write the following OCaml function that returns the string representation of a shape:

```
(* OCaml *)
let rec shape_to_string s = match s with
                            | Circle r -> "circle"
                            | Rectangle _ -> "rectangle"
```

But the OCaml compiler gives the following warning message:

```
(* OCaml *)
Lines 1-3, characters 28-63:
```

4 COMPOUND DATA TYPES

```
3  Warning 8: this pattern-matching is not
       exhaustive.
4  Here is an example of a case that is not
       matched:
5  ComplexShape _
6  val shape_to_string : shape -> string = <fun>
```

What is the OCaml compiler trying to tell us?

Please select all following choices that apply.

Choice A: Our code has syntax errors

Choice B: Our code is error-prone because we forget to match the pattern `ComplexShape`.

4.7.6 Quiz 6

Given the following function f in OCaml:

```
1  (* OCaml *)
2  let f l =
3    let rec aux l = match l with
4                    | [] -> ""
5                    | hd :: [] -> string_of_int hd
6                    | hd :: tl -> (string_of_int hd)
                         ^ "; " ^ (aux tl)
7    in "[" ^ (aux l) ^ "]"
```

What are the values of the following function applications?

```
1  (* OCaml *)
2  f [] = ?
3  f [1] = ?
4  f [1; 2] = ?
```

4 COMPOUND DATA TYPES

Please select all following choices that apply.

Choice A:

```
1  f [] = ""
2  f [1] = "1"
3  f [1; 2] = "1; 2"
```

Choice B:

```
1  f [] = "[]"
2  f [1] = "[1]"
3  f [1; 2] = "[1; 2]"
```

Choice C:

```
1  f [] = ""
2  f [1] = "[1]"
3  f [1; 2] = "[1;2]"
```

4.7.7 Quiz 7

Given the following OCaml function:

```
1  (* OCaml *)
2  let f n l = Option.map String.length (List.nth_opt l n)
```

Where,

- Option.map: ('a -> 'b)-> 'a option -> 'b option maps an option to a new option using a function.
- List.nth_opt: 'a list -> int -> 'a option returns the n-th element of a list if exists and None otherwise.

4 COMPOUND DATA TYPES

The head of the list is at position 0.
- `String.length: string -> int` returns the length of a string.

What are the values of the following expressions?

```
1  f 0 [] = ?
2  f 0 ["Hello"] = ?
3  f 1 ["Hello"; "Bye"] = ?
```

Please select all following choices that apply.

Choice A:

```
1  f 0 [] = None
2  f 0 ["Hello"] = Some 5
3  f 1 ["Hello"; "Bye"] = Some 3
```

Choice B:

```
1  f 0 [] = 0
2  f 0 ["Hello"] = 5
3  f 1 ["Hello"; "Bye"] = 3
```

4.7.8 Quiz 8

The following algebraic datatype defines natural numbers:

```
1  (* OCaml *)
2  type nat = Zero | Succ of nat
```

We define a the following function f on nat:

```
1  (* OCaml *)
2  let rec f n = match n with
```

4 COMPOUND DATA TYPES

```
3        | Zero -> ""
4        | Succ Zero -> "/"
5        | Succ n -> "/ " ^ (f n)
```

What are the values of the following expressions?

```
1  f Zero = ?
2  f (Succ Zero) = ?
3  f (Succ (Succ Zero)) = ?
```

Please select all following choices that apply.

Choice A:

```
1  f Zero = 0
2  f (Succ Zero) = 1
3  f (Succ (Succ Zero)) = 2
```

Choice B:

```
1  f Zero = ""
2  f (Succ Zero) = "/"
3  f (Succ (Succ Zero)) = "//"
```

Choice C:

```
1  f Zero = ""
2  f (Succ Zero) = "/"
3  f (Succ (Succ Zero)) = "/ /"
```

4   COMPOUND DATA TYPES

4.8 Answers to Quiz on Compound Datatypes

4.8.1 Quiz 1

Choice B is correct. The type `string * int * bool` contains all triples whose first element is a string, the second an integer, and the third is a boolean value. For instance, `("Hi", 0, true)` and `("Bye", 100, false)` are elements of that type. It is easy to see that the number of possible elements is infinite.

4.8.2 Quiz 2

Choice A is correct. The algebraic data type `mytype` has two data constructors. The first constructor `BoolVal of bool` can produce two different values `BoolVal true` and `BoolVal false`. The second constructor is a constant and hence is a single element. In total, this type contains 3 different values.

4.8.3 Quiz 3

Choice A is correct. The function `safe_hd` extracts the head of a list, similar to `List.hd`. The difference is it uses the `option` type as the return type because the head does not exist in the case of an empty list.

4 COMPOUND DATA TYPES

4.8.4 Quiz 4

Choice B is correct. Lists in OCaml or other functional programming languages are immutable. That means we cannot modify a list once created.

To obtain the list `["John"; "Adam"; "Anna"]`, we need to create an entirely new list from the original list. The following shows one way to do this in OCaml.

```
(* OCaml *)
let l = ["Joe"; "Adam"; "Anna"]
"John" :: (List.tl l)
```

4.8.5 Quiz 5

Choice B is correct. The OCaml type checker can infer that we are pattern matching the `shape` algebraic data type. And since `shape` has 3 data constructors, it expects 3 patterns to be matched. However, since our code provides only 2 patterns, a warning is issued. This is a helpful feature because the compiler catches this kind of human error at compile time.

4.8.6 Quiz 6

Choice B is correct. The `aux` function concatenates the string representation of list elements recursively. Notice that there is an empty space after the delimiter ;.

4 COMPOUND DATA TYPES

4.8.7 Quiz 7

Choice A is correct. Here, `List.nth_opt` returns the n-th string of a string list in an `option` type. Then, we use `Option.map` to maps the resulting string to its length. That means, f's return type is `option`.

4.8.8 Quiz 8

Choice C is correct. The function f turns a `nat` into a string representation. If a `nat` represents a natural number n, the resulting string contains n backslashes separated by an empty space.

5 Common Computation Patterns

5.1 The map Function

The map function is one of the most popular abstractions in the functional programming paradigm. It is best known for mapping the elements of a list to new elements. Due to its usefulness, map has found its way into most mainstream programming languages such as JavaScript, Java, and Python.

5.1.1 The map function on lists

One way of looking at map on lists is that it represents a general method of computation on lists. First, let's write a function square_list that squares all elements in a list to see what that pattern is.

```
(* OCaml *)
let rec square_list l =
  match l with
  | [] -> []
  | hd :: tl -> (hd * hd) :: square_list tl

square_list [1; 2; 3]
(* Result: [1; 4; 9] *)
```

Let's write another function called cube_list that turns the elements of a list into their cube.

```
(* OCaml *)
let rec cube_list l =
  match l with
```

5 COMMON COMPUTATION PATTERNS

```
4    | [] -> []
5    | hd :: tl -> (hd * hd * hd) :: cube_list tl
6
7  cube_list [1; 2; 3]
8  (* Result: [1; 4; 9] *)
```

The implementations of `square_list` and `cube_list` are strikingly similar. The differences between these functions lie in their last lines that compute the head of the output list from the head of the input list, hd * hd vs. hd * hd * hd. Other than that, the shape of the functions looks identical.

As we have seen multiple times in the this, this kind of common shape is almost always an opportunity to climb up the abstraction hierarchy. We can factor out the common pattern into a higher-order `map` function that takes an `f` function and a list as input. It then applies `f` uniformly to all list elements and produces a new list containing the resulting elements. The two functions, `square_list` and `cube_list`, become particular cases of `map`.

```
1  (* OCaml *)
2  let square_list = map (fun x -> x * x)
3  let cube_list = map (fun x -> x * x * x)
```

The following diagram illustrates this abstraction process:

5 COMMON COMPUTATION PATTERNS

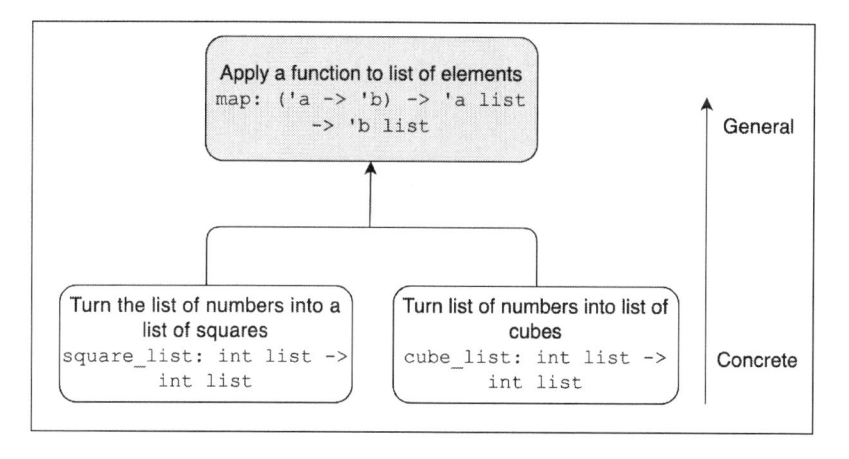

Figure 47: 'map' as a general method of computation on list

What makes map such a powerful abstraction is that it allows us to treat the transformation of a sequence of data as a high-level concept. With map, we focus on what transformation is rather than what the transformation step looks like.

Another excellent way to understand `map f l` is to view it as replacing each element `e` of the list `l` with `f e`, as depicted below:

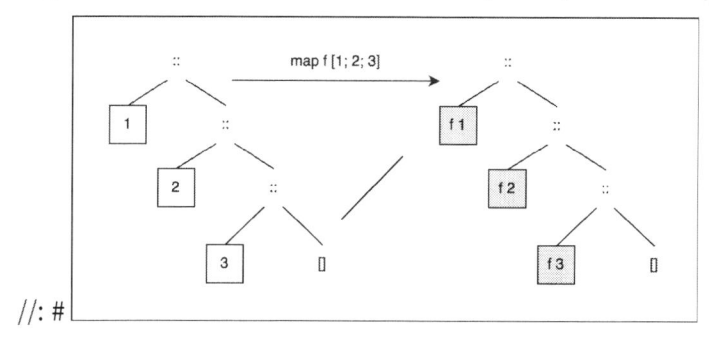

//: #

The Art of Functional Programming 175

5 COMMON COMPUTATION PATTERNS

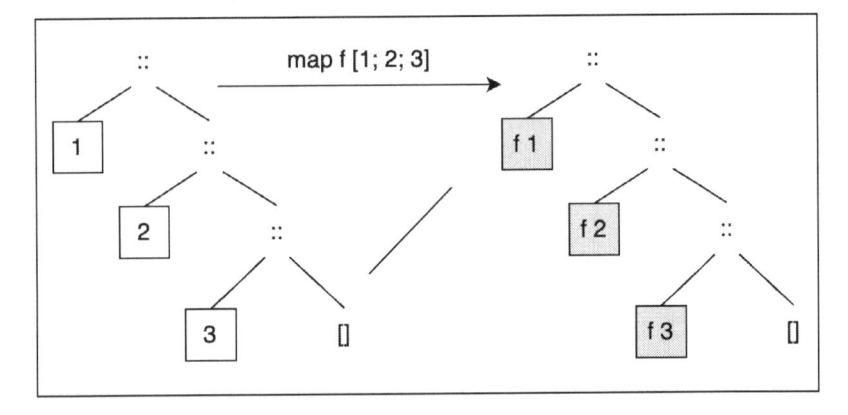

Figure 48: 'map' replaces each element 'e' with 'f e'

The OCaml module List includes `map: ('a -> 'b) -> 'a list -> 'b list`, which does exactly what we described above.

```
(* OCaml *)
List.map (fun x -> x * x) [1; 2; 3]
(* Result: [1; 4; 9] *)
```

5.1.2 The map function on trees

The map concept generalizes to hierarchical data structures, especially when they contain elements of the same type. To illustrate, let's define a map function for the binary tree with the following algebraic data type.

```
(* OCaml *)
type 'a bin_tree = Leaf | Node of 'a bin_tree
    * 'a * 'a bin_tree
```

5 COMMON COMPUTATION PATTERNS

A binary tree is either a `Leaf` with no fields or a `Node` containing a left node, the data, and a right node. The following figure shows an example of a binary tree.

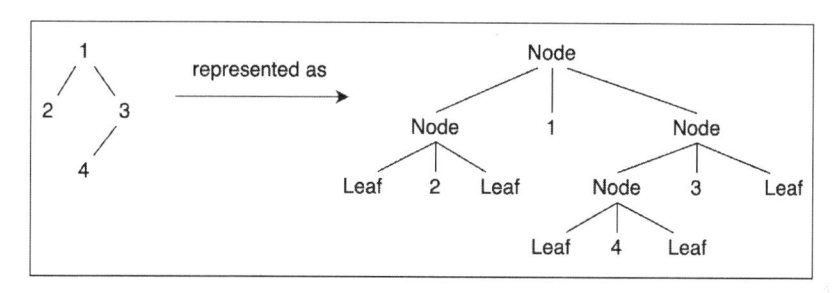

Figure 49: An example of binary tree

The example binary tree in the figure above is represented in OCaml, as shown below:

```
(* OCaml *)
Node (Node (Leaf, 2, Leaf), 1, Node (Node (
    Leaf, 4, Leaf), 3, Leaf))
```

We can define a `map` function that takes a function `f` and a binary tree `t` as arguments, and then applies `f` uniformly to the data of each tree node.

```
(* OCaml *)
let rec map_tree f t =
  match t with
  | Leaf -> Leaf
  | Node (l, v, r) -> Node (map_tree f l, f v,
      map_tree f r)
```

Similar to `map` on lists, we can view `map_tree f t` as replacing the

5 COMMON COMPUTATION PATTERNS

data e of a node with f e.

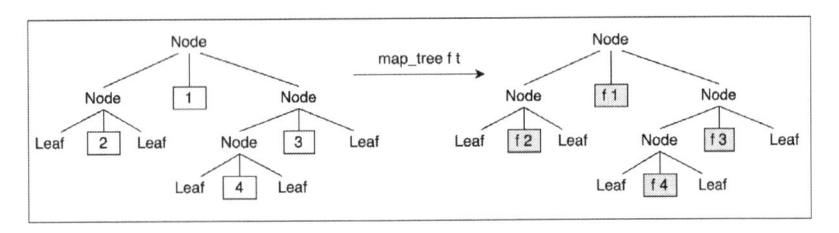

Figure 50: 'map_tree' replaces each node's value e with f e

We use `map_tree` to square all tree elements by passing a square function (`fun x -> x * x`).

```
(* OCaml *)
map_tree (fun x -> x * x) (Node (Node (Leaf,
    2, Leaf), 1, Node (Node (Leaf, 4, Leaf),
    3, Leaf)))
(* Result: Node (Node (Leaf, 4, Leaf), 1, Node
    (Node (Leaf, 16, Leaf), 9, Leaf)) *)
```

Additionally, we can map all node elements of the tree to their cube using a cube function, `fun x -> x * x * x`.

```
(* OCaml *)
map_tree (fun x -> x * x * x) (Node (Node (
    Leaf, 2, Leaf), 1, Node (Node (Leaf, 4,
    Leaf), 3, Leaf)))
(* Result: Node (Node (Leaf, 8, Leaf), 1, Node
    (Node (Leaf, 64, Leaf), 27, Leaf)) *)
```

5 COMMON COMPUTATION PATTERNS

5.1.3 The map function on containers

Lists or binary trees from the previous sections are examples of containers – data structures that contain elements. As it turns out, we can often define a meaningful map function for a container type. For example, OCaml's option type is a container type.

```
(* OCaml *)
type 'a option = None | Some of 'a
```

The `option` container is either empty (`None`) or contains a value x (`Some x`).

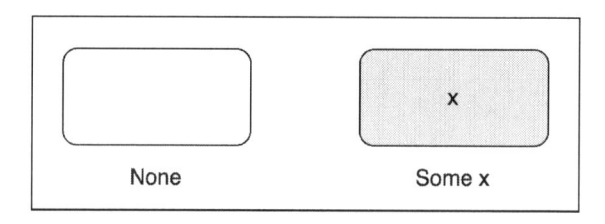

Figure 51: 'option' type as container

We can define a map function for the option type.

```
(* OCaml *)
let map_option f o = match o with
                    | None -> None
                    | Some x -> Some (f x)

map_option (fun x -> x * x) None
(* Result: None *)
map_option (fun x -> x * x) (Some 3)
(* Result: Some 9 *)
```

5 COMMON COMPUTATION PATTERNS

We can think of `map_option f o` as replacing the data `x` inside `Some` with `f x` while doing nothing for `None`, as shown in the following diagram.

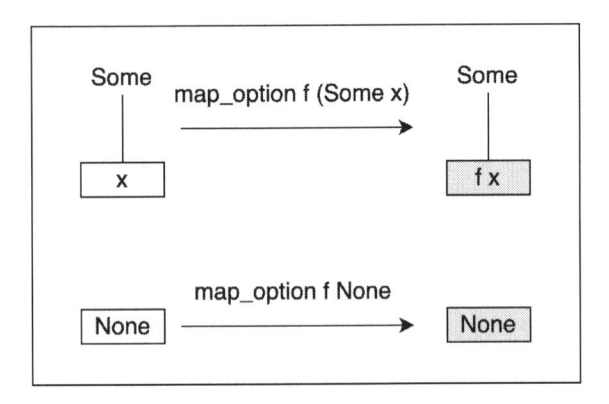

Figure 52: 'map_option' replaces 'x' inside 'Some' with 'f x'

The OCaml `Option` module provides a `map` function for the `option` type that behaves exactly like `map_option` above.

```
(* OCaml *)
Option.map (fun x -> x * x) None
(* Result: None *)
Option.map (fun x -> x * x) (Some 3)
(* Result: Some 9 *)
```

The ability to map over `option` is very useful for error handling. For example, we can use it to implement the following function `longest_string: 'a list -> 'a option` function. This function finds the longest string in a list.

```
(* OCaml *)
let rec longest_string l =
```

5 COMMON COMPUTATION PATTERNS

```
3      match l with
4      | [] -> None
5      | hd :: tl ->
6        let s = longest_string tl in
7            match s with
8            | None -> Some hd
9            | Some x -> if String.length
                         hd > String.length x then
                         Some hd else Some x
10
11    longest_string []
12    (* Result: None *)
13    longest_string ["a"; "abc"; "ab"]
14    (* Result: Some "abc" *)
```

Here, the function returns an `option` type because the longest string does not exist for an empty list.

What if we want to write a `max_length` function that returns the length of the longest string in a list? We compose `longest_string` with `Option.map`.

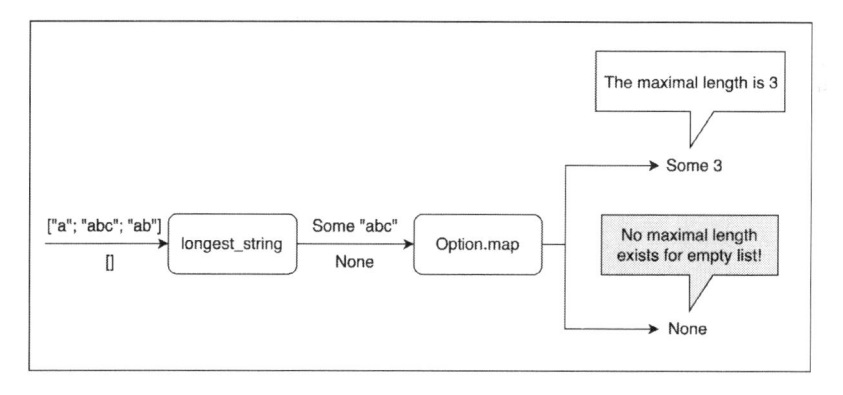

Figure 53: Compose 'longest_string' with 'Option.map'

5 COMMON COMPUTATION PATTERNS

We can express that in OCaml, as shown below:

```ocaml
(* OCaml *)
let max_length l = Option.map String.length (
    longest_string l)

max_length []
(* Result: None *)
max_length ["a"; "abc"; "ab"]
(* Result: Some 3 *)
```

Thanks to the way `Option.map` is defined, we can handle two cases simultaneously. If the longest string exists, we map it to its length. Otherwise, we return an empty result.

Next, let's look at how `map` transforms data for list, tree and `option`.

5 COMMON COMPUTATION PATTERNS

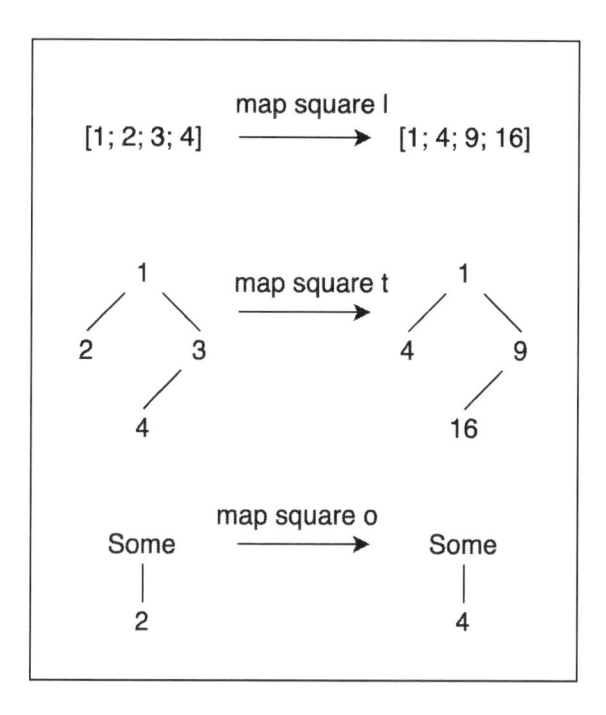

```
                    map square l
     [1; 2; 3; 4]   ─────────▶   [1; 4; 9; 16]


            1        map square t        1
           / \       ─────────▶         / \
          2   3                        4   9
              /                            /
             4                            16


                    map square o
         Some       ─────────▶       Some
          |                           |
          2                           4
```

Figure 54: 'map' preserves the container's structure

The diagram above clearly shows that map applies a function to each container's element without altering the container's structure. This is one of the critical properties a map abstraction must satisfy. When we formulate map for another container type, we should definitely keep this in mind.

5.1.4 The map function on domains or contexts

A map function is a highly general and reusable concept that extends beyond regular containers, such as list, tree, and option. In fact, we

5 COMMON COMPUTATION PATTERNS

can generalize `map` to the mapping between domains or contexts. This becomes evident when we examine the type signature of `map`.

```
1  List.map: ('a -> 'b) -> 'a list -> 'b list
2  map_tree: ('a -> 'b) -> 'a bin_tree -> 'b
     bin_tree
3  Option.map: ('a -> 'b) -> 'a option -> 'b
     option
```

The three type signatures share an underlying common pattern. That means we can climb up the abstraction hierarchy by generalizing `map` to (`'a -> 'b`)-> `'a context -> 'b context` where `context` is some type.

The following diagram shows this generalization process:

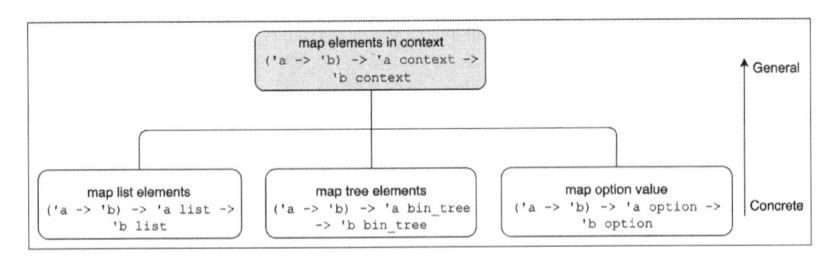

Figure 55: 'map' is a general computation on domain or context

A `context` can either be a container type, like list, or an abstract concept such as asynchronous computation. Suppose we define a type `future` that encapsulates an asynchronous computation that returns a value at some point. In this case, we can formulate a `map_future` function that maps a `future` to another `future` by applying a function to the value of the former `future`.

5 COMMON COMPUTATION PATTERNS

```
1  map_future: ('a -> 'b) -> 'a future -> 'b
     future
```

That is precisely the idea behind the `map` function defined in `Future` in the Scala programming language. In particular, `Future.map` allows us to map values computed by an asynchronous computation without knowing how the computation is carried out.

Recall we mentioned that `map` on a container does not change the container's structure. Similarly, a `map` for a domain/context should apply a function to a value without altering the context. For instance, `Future.map` can map the value held by a `Future` instance. Still, it should not change the asynchronous computation represented by that `Future` instance.

5.1.5 map as lifting function

Another powerful way to look at `map` is as a lifting function. To see what it means, suppose we've defined a function `square` that takes as an argument an integer and returns its square. To define the `square` concept for a context, such as list, tree, optional value, or even asynchronous computation, we can use `map` to lift `square` to that domain.

For instance, if we partially apply `List.map: ('a -> 'b)-> 'a list -> 'b list` to the function `square: int -> int`, we obtain a function `int list-> int list` that knows how to square list elements. In general, `map` can be thought of as lifting a `'a -> 'b` function to a `'a context -> 'b context` function. It's capa-

The Art of Functional Programming

5 COMMON COMPUTATION PATTERNS

ble of mapping one context to another.

The following diagram visualizes map as a lifting function worldview.

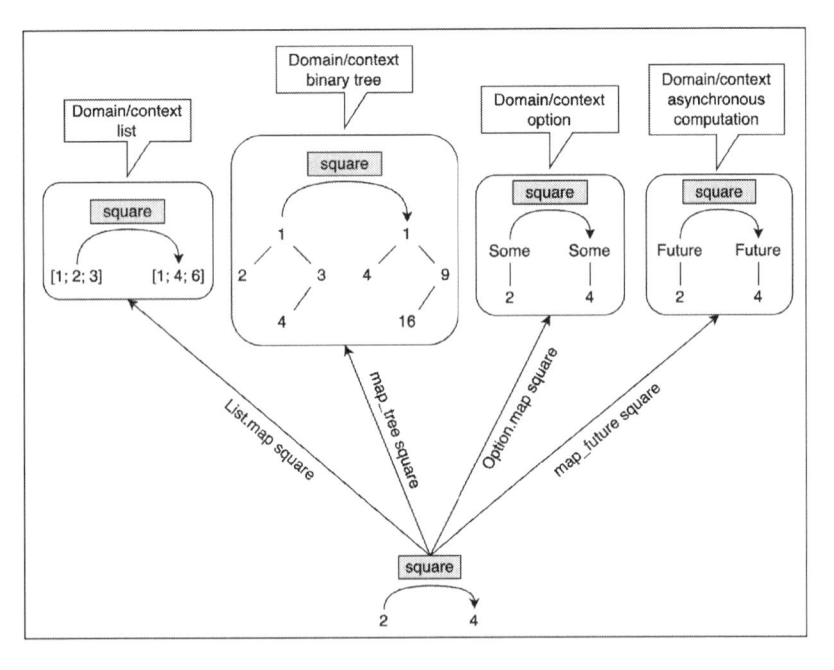

Figure 56: 'map' lifts a function to a new domain or context

The takeaway of this section is that map is a highly general method of computation. It allows us to think about data transformation for a structure as a conceptual unit. We don't need to care about how the mapping is done for each element individually.

5 COMMON COMPUTATION PATTERNS

5.2 The filter function

Another crucial function abstraction is `filter`. We can use it to filter out the elements of a list based on a given condition.

5.2.1 The `filter` function on lists

Let's write a function `evens` that returns only even numbers from an integer list.

```
(* OCaml *)
let rec evens l =
    match l with
    | [] -> []
    | hd :: tl -> if even hd then hd :: evens
        tl else evens tl

evens [1; 2; 3; 4; 5]
(* Result: [2; 4] *)
```

We write another function, `positives`, that return only positive numbers from a list of integers.

```
(* OCaml *)
let rec positives l =
    match l with
    | [] -> []
    | hd :: tl -> if positive hd then hd ::
        positives tl else positives tl

positives [-1; 0; 1; 2; -3; 4]
(* Result: [1; 2; 4] *)
```

Obviously, `evens` and `positives` share a common pattern. The

5 COMMON COMPUTATION PATTERNS

real difference is the function that checks the head of the list and decides whether it belongs to the result or not. We can factor out the common pattern as a higher-order function called `filter`, which accepts a function making a filtering decision as an argument.

The following diagram shows how we climb up the abstraction hierarchy by formulating `filter` as a general method of computation.

```
Filtering out elements in a list based on a
                predicate
filter: ('a -> bool) -> 'a list ->
                a' list
```
General

```
Filtering out even numbers        Filtering out positive numbers
        in a list                            in a list
evens: int list ->                positives: int list ->
       int list                              int list
```
Concrete

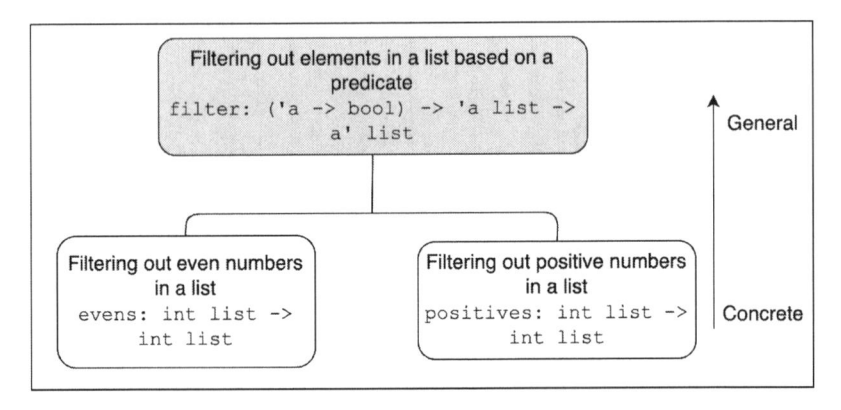

Figure 57: 'filter' as a general computation pattern on list

In OCaml,

```ocaml
(* OCaml *)
let rec filter p l =
    match l with
    | [] -> []
    | hd :: tl -> if p hd then hd :: filter p tl else filter p tl
```

Notice that p returns a boolean value as a result. Such a function is called a **predicate**. The helper functions, even, positive, are all

The Art of Functional Programming   188

5 COMMON COMPUTATION PATTERNS

predicates.

Now we can easily formulate `evens` and `positives` in terms of `filter`.

```
(* OCaml *)
let even x = x mod 2 = 0
filter even [1; 2; 3; 4]
(* Result: [2; 4] *)

let positive x = x > 0
filter positive [-1; 0; 1; 2; -3; 4]
(* Result: [1; 2; 4] *)
```

The `List` module of OCaml provides the same `filter` function described above.

```
(* OCaml *)
List.filter even [1; 2; 3; 4]
(* Result: [2; 4] *)

List.filter positive [-1; 0; 1; 2; -3; 4]
(* Result: [1; 2; 4] *)
```

In general, the concept of `filter` applies most naturally to a collection of data. For instance, we can also define a `filter` function for a set data structure, that contains elements without particular order. It filters out the set elements based on a given predicate.

5.2.2 Compose predicates

What if we write a function, `odds`, that returns odd numbers from a list? We can define a predicate, `odd`, and pass it to `filter`.

5 COMMON COMPUTATION PATTERNS

```
(* OCaml *)
let odd x = x mod 2 <> 0
let odds = List.filter odd
```

Or we can even pass an anonymous predicate directly as an argument to `filter`.

```
(* OCaml *)
List.filter (fun x -> x mod 2 <> 0) [1; 2; 3;
    4; 5]
```

In either case, we have to define a new predicate to check an odd number, which is less than ideal. We already have a predicate, `even`. It would be better to reuse `even` to formulate `odd` because, by definition, an odd number is not an even number.

In fact, OCaml already provides a `not` predicate that negates a boolean value. That means the predicate to check whether a number is odd or not is simply a function composition of `not` and `even`. We define a `compose` function for composing two other functions as follows:

```
(* OCaml *)
let compose f g x = f (g x)
```

With that, the function `odds` for returning all odd numbers of a list can be formulated in OCaml as follows.

```
(* OCaml *)
let odds = List.filter (compose not even)

odds [1; 2; 3; 4]
(* Result: [1; 3] *)
```

5 COMMON COMPUTATION PATTERNS

Analogously, we can define a `negatives_or_zero` function that returns all numbers less or equal 0 from a list.

```
(* OCaml *)
let negatives_or_zero = List.filter (compose
    not positive)

negatives_or_zero [-1; 0; 1; 2; -3; 4]
(* Result: [-1; 0; -3] *)
```

As you can see, `filter` allows us to treat the filtering of a list as a single concept rather than rather than needing to work with each list element individually. This allows us to think on a high level when writing programs. Given its usefulness, it is no surprise that most mainstream programming languages such as Java, JavaScript, and Python support some form of `filter`.

5.3 The fold function

5.3.1 The fold function on lists

Often, we need to combine the list elements into a single value. For example, given a list, we might want to calculate the sum or the product of its elements. Such a computation pattern can be realized in the functional paradigm through a powerful function abstraction called `fold`.

Let's define a function, `sum_list`, to calculate the sum of all numbers from a list of integers.

```
(* OCaml *)
let rec sum_list l = match l with
```

5 COMMON COMPUTATION PATTERNS

```
| [] -> 0
| hd :: tl -> hd + sum_list tl

sum_list [1; 2; 3; 4]
(* Result: 10 *)
```

Next, let's define another function, `prod_list`, that returns the product of all numbers from a list.

```
(* OCaml *)
let rec prod_list l = match l with
  | [] -> 1
  | hd :: tl -> hd * prod_list tl

prod_list [1; 2; 3; 4]
(* Result: 24 *)
```

The `sum_list` and `prod_list` functions follow the same computation pattern.

- In case of an empty list `[]`, return an initial value, 0 for `sum_list`, and 1 for `prod_list`.
- For a `hd :: tl` list, apply a binary function f to hd, and the result for recursively processed `tl`. The function is addition + for `sum_list`, and multiplication * for `prod_list`.

This computation pattern is precisely what `fold_right` captures. We'll see in a minute why it is called `fold_right`. There is another fold version called `fold_left`, but we'll cover it later.

```
(* OCaml *)
let rec fold_right f init l =
  match l with
  | [] -> init
  | hd :: tl -> f hd (fold_right f init tl)
```

The Art of Functional Programming

5 COMMON COMPUTATION PATTERNS

Here, `f` is the function used to combine the list elements, `init` is the initial value. The last argument `l` is the input list.

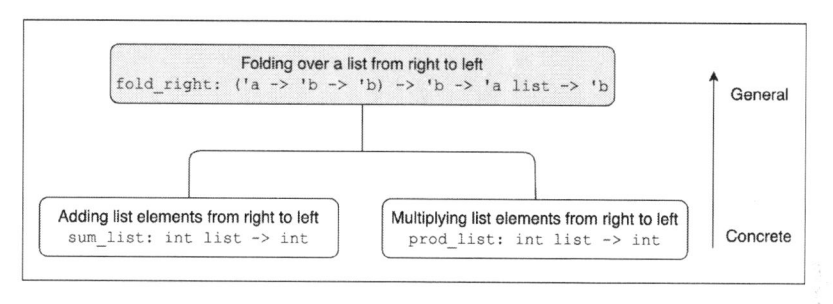

Figure 58: Computation pattern for folding lists

This function is called `fold_right` because the way it works is visually similar to how we fold clothes. In particular, we fold the list from right to left, one element at a time, until the whole list collapses into one element.

An easy way is to think of `fold_right f init` is as replacing the empty list `[]` with the initial value `init` and the list constructor `::` with `f`.

5 COMMON COMPUTATION PATTERNS

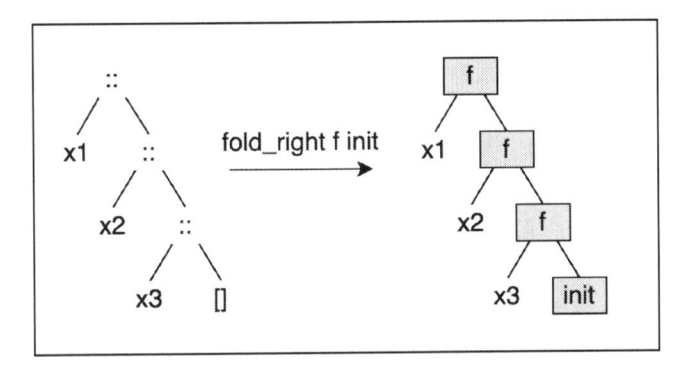

Figure 59: 'fold_right' as constructor replacement

If the initial value `init` is 0 and the binary function f adds two integers, `fold_right (+) 0` sums up all elements in the list.

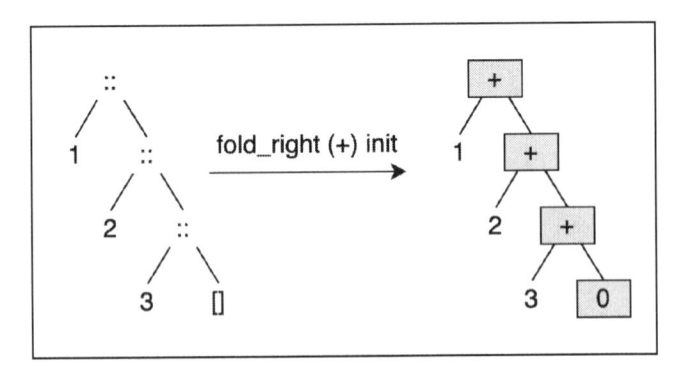

Figure 60: Fold over a list using addition

In other words, we can readily formulate `sum_list`, and `product_list` as a special cases of `fold_right`, as shown below:

5 COMMON COMPUTATION PATTERNS

```
(* OCaml *)
let sum_list = fold_right (+) 0
let prod_list = fold_right ( * ) 1
```

The `List` module of OCaml provides a `fold_right` function. But it's important to note that `List.fold_right`: `('a -> 'b -> 'b)-> 'a list -> 'b -> 'b` has a slightly different type than the one we defined earlier. `List.fold_right` accepts the initial value as the last parameter instead of a list. This may be not a good idea because it prevents us from connecting `List.fold_right` with other functions. Haskell's built-in function `foldr` has a similar type as our version.

The `fold` function is a truly powerful abstraction that can be used to formulate many other useful functions on lists. For example, a handy function, found in many languages, notably JavaScript or Python, is `any`: `bool list -> bool`. It takes as input a list of `bool` and returns **true** if any element in the list is **true**. Otherwise, it returns **false**, as we can see below:

```
(* OCaml *)
any [true; false; false] = true
any [false; false; false] = false
```

We can easily formulate `any` using `fold_right` by configuring the folding function to the logical `OR` function (`||`) and the initial value to **false**.

```
(* OCaml *)
let any l = List.fold_right (||) l false
```

Likewise, we can formulate the function `all`: `bool list ->`

The Art of Functional Programming

bool that returns **true** if all elements in the input list are **true** and **false** otherwise.

```
(* OCaml *)
let all l = List.fold_right (&&) l true

all [true; true; true]
(* Result: true *)
all [true; false; false]
(* Result: false *)
```

An interesting use case is using `fold_right` to formulate a `length` function to calculate the length of a list. The key idea is that we start with the length 0 for the case of empty list []. When we encounter a list constructor :: at each folding step, we increase the accumulative length by 1.

```
(* OCaml *)
let length l = List.fold_right (fun x len ->
    len + 1) l 0;;

length [1; 2; 3]
(* Result: 3 *)
```

In fact, `fold` is so powerful that `map` can be seen as one of its particular use case.

```
(* OCaml *)
let map f l = List.fold_right (fun x l -> f x
    :: l) l []

map (fun x -> x * x) [1; 2; 3]
(* Result: [1; 4; 9] *)
```

What's interesting here is that `fold_right` reconstructs the input list and applies the mapping function `f` to its head to transform its head.

In mainstream programming languages, `fold` is often known by another name, for example, `reduce` in Python or Java. Regardless of the term, the idea is the same—we use a combining function to accumulate all list elements into a value, starting with an initial value. The higher-order function abstractions, `map`, `fold`, and `reduce`, inspired the popular Google framework for parallel processing of large data sets called MapReduce with Apache Hadoop– a popular open-source implementation.

5.3.2 The `fold` function on trees

The `fold` function generalizes naturally to hierarchical data structures such as trees. To illustrate, we'll define fold on a binary tree. For that, we'll use the following algebraic data type to represent a binary tree.

```
type 'a bin_tree = Leaf | Node of 'a bin_tree
    * 'a * 'a bin_tree
```

The general strategy to design the `fold` function is to replace the data constructors with functions `f` and constants with an initial value `init`. In the case of the binary tree, we could substitute `Node` with a 3-argument function `f`, and `Leaf` with an initial value `init`. The following diagram visualizes this idea.

5 COMMON COMPUTATION PATTERNS

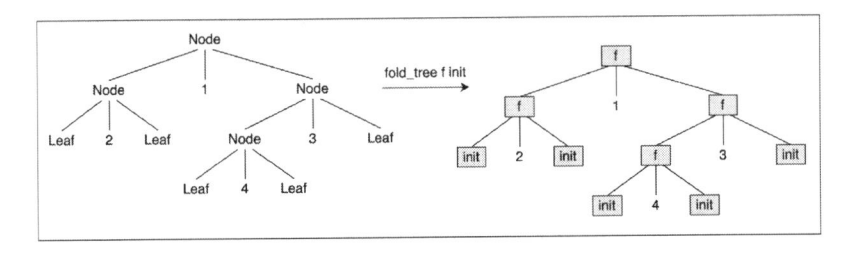

Figure 61: Fold a binary tree

The diagram above translates to the following OCaml code.

```
(* OCaml *)
let rec fold_tree f init t =
  match t with
  | Leaf -> init
  | Node (l, x, r) -> f (fold_tree f init l)
      x (fold_tree f init r)
```

Instead of defining many functions for the binary tree from scratch, we can reuse the folding a tree computation. For instance, summing up all integers in a tree of integer nodes is just a use case of `fold_tree`.

```
(* OCaml *)
let sum_tree = fold_tree (fun suml x sumr ->
    suml + x + sumr) 0

sum_tree (Node (Node (Leaf, 2, Leaf), 1, Node
    (Node (Leaf, 4, Leaf), 3, Leaf))))
(* Result: 10 *)
```

Similarly, we can use `fold_tree` to formulate a function that calculates the size of the tree. The size here refers to the number of nodes.

5 COMMON COMPUTATION PATTERNS

```
(* OCaml *)
let size t = fold_tree (fun suml x sumr ->
    suml + 1 + sumr) 0 t

size (Node (Node (Leaf, 2, Leaf), 1, Node (
    Node (Leaf, 4, Leaf), 3, Leaf)))
(* Result: 4 *)
```

To collect all tree elements into a list, we use another use case of `fold_tree`.

```
(* OCaml *)
let tree_elements = fold_tree (fun l x r -> [x
    ] @ l @ r) []

tree_elements (Node (Node (Leaf, 2, Leaf), 1,
    Node (Node (Leaf, 4, Leaf), 3, Leaf)))
(* Result: [1; 2; 3; 4] *)
```

5.3.3 The fold function on other data types

The `fold` concept can be defined for many types. For instance, we'll define the `fold` function for the `option` type and an algebraic data type representing naturals.

Option type

Recall that the `option` type is defined as an algebraic data type, as shown below:

```
type 'a option = None | Some of 'a
```

We can define a `fold` function for this type. The following OCaml function, `fold_option`, replaces `None` with an initial value `init` and `Some x` with `f x`.

```
(* OCaml *)
let fold_option f init o = match o with
                          | None -> init
                          | Some x -> f x

fold_option (fun x -> x * x) 42 None
(* Result: 42 *)

fold_option (fun x -> x * x) 42 (Some 3)
(* Result: 9 *)
```

Naturals

We can represent natural numbers using the following algebraic data type:

```
(* OCaml *)
type nat = Zero | Succ of nat
```

According to this definition, the integer number 4 is represented as `Succ (Succ (Succ (Succ Zero)))`

We can also define a `fold` function for `nat` – one that replaces `Zero` with an initial value and `Succ` with an `f` function as graphically depicted below:

5 COMMON COMPUTATION PATTERNS

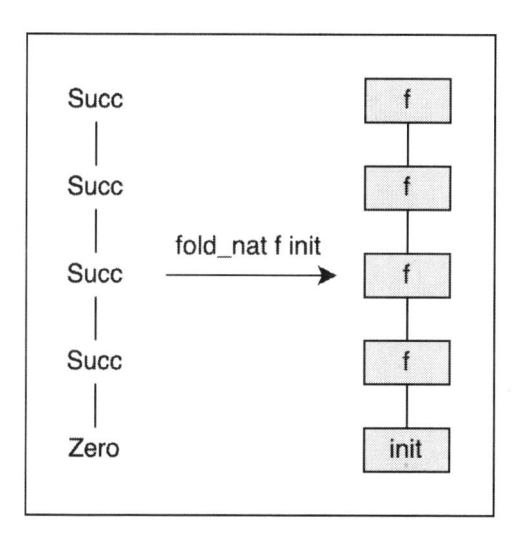

Figure 62: 'fold' on naturals

In OCaml code,

```ocaml
(* OCaml *)
let rec fold_nat f init n = match n with
                            | Zero -> init
                            | Succ m -> f (
                                fold_nat f
                                init m)
```

In essence, `fold_nat f init n` computes `f(...f(init))` whereby `f` occurs n times.

We use `fold_nat` to formulate many useful functions on `nat`. For instance, we can define a function that converts a `nat` to the corresponding integer it represents. The idea is we fold `nat` using the incremental function `(+) 1` to count the number of `Succ`, while the initial value `0` is used for the case of `Zero`.

5 COMMON COMPUTATION PATTERNS

```ocaml
(* OCaml *)
let nat_to_int = fold_nat ((+) 1) 0

nat_to_int (Succ (Succ (Succ (Succ Zero))))
(* Result: 4 *)
```

We can also define a function that prints a `nat` as a string.

```ocaml
(* OCaml *)
let nat_to_string = fold_nat (fun x -> "Succ (
    " ^ x ^ ")") "Zero"

nat_to_string (Succ (Succ (Succ (Succ Zero))))
(* Result: "Succ (Succ (Succ (Succ (Zero))))"
   *)
```

The main takeaway from this section is that `fold` is a highly general function abstraction for various datatypes. It allows us to deal with data aggregation on a high level without caring about the details of how the aggregation is executed. It is often a good idea to consider designing a `fold` function for our data whenever we define a data structure, especially a recursive one.

5.4 The zip Function

5.4.1 `zip` two lists into list of pairs

Functions like `map`, `filter`, and `fold` have a limitation – they only work with a single list. What if we want to combine multiple lists?

In the functional paradigm, there is another powerful function abstraction called `zip`. One form of `zip` takes two input lists and re-

5 COMMON COMPUTATION PATTERNS

turns a list of corresponding pairs. We can implement such a `zip` function in OCaml, as shown below:

```
(* OCaml *)
let rec zip l1 l2 = match l1, l2 with
                    | [], _ -> []
                    | _, [] -> []
                    | x :: xs, y :: ys -> (x,
                        y) :: zip xs ys

zip [1; 2; 3] [4; 5; 6]
(* Result: [(1, 4); (2, 5); (3, 6)] *)
```

Note that if we apply the `zip` function to two lists of different lengths, it simply ignores the additional elements of the longer list.

Let's apply `zip` to form a list of points in the 2D plane. Assume we have two lists `xcoords` and `ycoords` containing x and y coordinates, respectively. We can use `zip` to combine them to form a list of pairs denoting 2D points.

```
(* OCaml *)
let xcoords = [0.0; 1.0; 2.0]
let ycoords = [0.0; 2.0; 1.0]

let points = zip xcoords ycoords
(* Result: [(0., 0.); (1., 2.); (2., 1.)] *)
```

This function is called `zip` because the way it works resembles how a clothing zipper's teeth combine. In particular, we can imagine `zip` as zipping two lists into one.

5 COMMON COMPUTATION PATTERNS

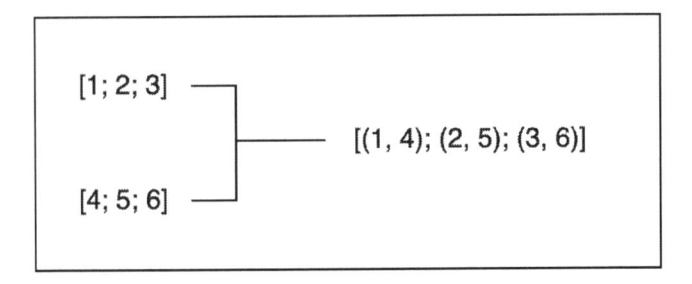

```
[1; 2; 3] ┐
          ├──── [(1, 4); (2, 5); (3, 6)]
[4; 5; 6] ┘
```

Figure 63: 'zip' two lists into one

5.4.2 zip two lists with function

We can generalize the `zip` function introduced in the previous section to `zipWith` by allowing it to accept a binary function f, in addition to two lists. It produces an output list whose elements result from applying f to the elements of the input lists. We can implement `zipWith` in OCaml as a higher-order function, as shown below:

```
(* OCaml *)
let rec zipWith f l1 l2 = match l1, l2 with
                          | [], _ -> []
                          | _, [] -> []
                          | x :: xs, y :: ys
                            -> f x y ::
                               zipWith f xs ys
```

The `zip` function is just a particular use case of `zipWith`, where the function f constructs a pair from two elements. The following OCaml code defines `zip` as a particular case of `zipWith`:

```
(* OCaml *)
```

5 COMMON COMPUTATION PATTERNS

```
2  let zip l1 l2 = zipWith (fun x y -> (x, y)) l1
       l2
```

As a general-purpose higher-order function, we can use `zipWith` is to formulate other functions. For example, `zipWith (+)` accepts two lists and produces a new list of corresponding sums.

```
1  (* OCaml *)
2  zipWith (+) [1; 2; 3] [4; 5; 6]
3  (* Result: [5; 7; 9] *)
```

As another example, we can define a `square_list` function that squares all elements in a list. It uses multiplication to zip the input list with itself.

```
1  (* OCaml *)
2  let square_list l = zipWith ( * ) l l
3
4  square_list [1; 2; 3]
5  (* Result: [1; 4; 9] *)
```

We can use `zip` or `zipWith` to solve many programming tasks. Consider the problem of producing a new list containing the difference of adjacent elements in a given list. For example, for the input `[1; 9; 100; 37]`, the output should be `[8; 91; -63]`. This is because the difference between the second and first element is 9 - 1 = 8, the difference between the third and second element is 100 - 9 = 91, and so on.

An elegant solution is to use subtraction (-) as a combining function to zip the tail of the input list with the input. In OCaml, this looks like the following:

5 COMMON COMPUTATION PATTERNS

```ocaml
(* OCaml *)
let diff l = zipWith (-) (List.tl l) l

diff [1; 9; 100; 37]
(* Result: [8; 91; -63] *)
```

What if we want to write a function `total_abs_diff`, to calculate the sum of the absolute difference of adjacent elements of a given list. That is, the output of applying `total_abs_diff` to [1; 9; 100; 37] should be 8 + 91 + 63 = 162. We simply compose `zipWith` with `map` with `fold_right`.

```ocaml
(* OCaml *)
let total_abs_diff l = List.fold_right (+) (
    List.map abs (diff l)) 0

total_abs_diff [1; 9; 100; 37]
(* Result: 162 *)
```

The takeaway from this section is that `zip` is a general computation for combining multiple lists into a single one. Due to its usefulness, this abstraction has gained popularity in mainstream programming languages, such as Kotlin and Python.

5.5 Programming Challenges

Let's solve coding challenges to practice common computation patterns.

5 COMMON COMPUTATION PATTERNS

5.5.1 Challenge 1: map on `either` type

The following algebraic data type defines the `either` type:

```
(* OCaml *)
type ('a, 'b) either = Left of 'a | Right of 'b
```

As a convention, `Right of 'b` holds the correct (right) value while `Left of 'a` represents an error value.

Write a mapping function for `either` called `map_either : ('a -> 'b) -> ('c, 'a) either -> ('c, 'b) either`.

Examples:

```
map_either (fun x -> x * x) (Right 2) = Right 4
map_either (fun x -> x * x) (Left "Error case") = Left "Error case"
```

5.5.2 Challenge 2: `fold_left`

The function, `List.fold_right: ('a -> 'b -> 'b) -> 'a list -> 'b -> 'b`, folds a list from right to left. For example, `List.fold_right (-) [1; 2; 3] 0` calculates the expression $(1 - (2 - (3 - 0))) = -2$. Here, the initial value 0 is combined with the last element 3 of the list. We combine the result with the second to last element, which is 2, and so on.

If we fold a list from left to right, the expression would be $(((0 - 1) - 2) - 3) = -6$. The initial value 0 is combined with the first element 1. We combine the result with the second element and so on.

5 COMMON COMPUTATION PATTERNS

Write an OCaml function, `fold_left`: `('a -> 'b -> 'a)-> 'a -> 'b list -> 'a`, to fold the list from left to right. This function accepts a binary function f, an accumulator acc, and a list.

Examples:

```
(* OCaml *)
fold_left (-) 0 [1] = -1
fold_left (-) 0 [1; 2; 3] = -6
```

Beware that the `fold_left` has a different order of parameters as `List.fold_right`.

5.5.3 Challenge 3: Tree elements to list with `fold_tree`

The following algebraic data type defines a binary tree.

```
(* OCaml *)
type 'a bin_tree = Leaf | Node of 'a bin_tree
    * 'a * 'a bin_tree
```

We can define `fold_tree` : `('a -> 'b -> 'a -> 'a)-> 'a -> 'b bin_tree -> 'a` as a general function abstraction to fold over a tree.

```
(* OCaml *)
let rec fold_tree f init t =
    match t with
    | Leaf -> init
    | Node (l, x, r) -> f (fold_tree f init l)
        x (fold_tree f init r)
```

Write a function `tree_to_list`: `'a bin_tree -> 'a list` that collects all tree elements into a list by reusing `fold_tree`.

5 COMMON COMPUTATION PATTERNS

Examples:

```
(* OCaml *)
tree_to_list Leaf = []
tree_to_list (Node (Node (Leaf, 2, Leaf), 1,
    Node (Node (Leaf, 4, Leaf), 3, Leaf))) =
    [1; 2; 3; 4]
```

5.5.4 Challenge 4: Check an ascending list

The following higher-order `zipWith` function applies a function to two list's elements to zip them.

```
(* OCaml *)
let rec zipWith f l1 l2 =
    match l1, l2 with
    | [], _ -> []
    | _, [] -> []
    | x :: xs, y :: ys -> f x y :: zipWith f
        xs ys
```

Use `zipWith` to formulate a function, `is_ascending_sorted: int list -> bool`, that returns **true** if the input list is sorted in ascending order and **false** otherwise. A list may have duplicate values, and two adjacent equal elements are considered sorted.

Examples:

```
(* OCaml *)
is_ascending_sorted [1; 2; 3] = true
is_ascending_sorted [1; 1; 2] = true
is_ascending_sorted [3; 1; 2] = false
```

5.6 Solutions to Programming Challenges

5.6.1 Challenge 1: map on either type

The key idea is we only map the value inside the Right constructor. The Left constructor is intended to contain the error case and is therefore mapped to itself. The latter is conceptually similar to how we map None to None for the option type.

The following OCaml code shows a possible implementation for map_either.

```
(* OCaml *)
let map_either f e = match e with
                    | Left x -> Left x
                    | Right y -> Right (f y)
```

5.6.2 Challenge 2: fold_left

We can define a fold_left f acc l function, where acc accumulates the intermediate result during the recursive execution, as shown below:

```
(* OCaml *)
let rec fold_left f acc l =
    match l with
    | [] -> acc
    | hd :: tl -> fold_left f (f acc hd) tl
```

Notice that fold_left is a tail-recursive function. OCaml provides fold_left in the List module.

5 COMMON COMPUTATION PATTERNS

5.6.3 Challenge 3: Tree elements to list with `fold_tree`

We need to tell `fold_tree` what the initial value is and what the fold function looks like. The initial value is the empty list `[]`. The folding function concatenates the value of the node, the list of the left node, and the list of the right node into a list.

A possible solution in OCaml looks like following:

```
1  (* OCaml *)
2  let tree_to_list t = fold_tree (fun l x r -> [x] @ l @ r) [] t
```

5.6.4 Challenge 4: Check an ascending list

First, we define a function `all` that returns **true** if all boolean values in the list are **true** and **false** otherwise.

```
1  (* OCaml *)
2  let all l = List.fold_right (&&) l true
```

Then, we can use it in combination with `zipWith` to implement `is_ascending_sorted` as shown below:

```
1  (* OCaml *)
2  let is_ascending_sorted l = if l = [] then
        true else all (zipWith (<=) l (List.tl l))
```

5 COMMON COMPUTATION PATTERNS

5.7 Quiz on Common Computation Patterns

Let's test your understanding of the `map`, `filter`, `fold`, and `zip` functions.

5.7.1 Quiz 1

What is the output of the following function call?

```
1  (* OCaml *)
2  List.map ((+) 1) [1; 2; 3]
```

Please select all following choices that apply.

Choice A: `[1; 2; 3]`

Choice B: `[2; 3; 4]`

Choice C: `[4; 5; 6]`

5.7.2 Quiz 2

What is the type of `zipWith`?

Please select all following choices that apply.

Choice A: `('a -> 'b)-> 'a list -> 'b list -> 'c list`

Choice B: `('a -> 'b -> 'c)-> 'a list -> 'b list -> 'c list`

5 COMMON COMPUTATION PATTERNS

5.7.3 Quiz 3

Given the following list of pairs representing 2D points:

```
(* OCaml *)
let points = [(0., 0.); (1., 2.); (1.5, 3.5)]
```

What is the value of the following expression?

```
(* OCaml *)
List.map fst points
```

Please select all following choices that apply.

Choice A: `[0.; 1.; 1.5]`

Choice B: `[0.; 2.; 3.5]`

5.7.4 Quiz 4

Given the following function formulated using `List.fold_right`:

```
(* OCaml *)
let f p l = List.fold_right (fun x acc -> if p
    x then x :: acc else acc) l []
```

What does `f` do?

Please select all following choices that apply.

Choice A: It's a `filter` function which filters a list based on a given predicate.

Choice B: It copies a list

5   COMMON COMPUTATION PATTERNS

5.7.5 Quiz 5

Given the following OCaml function:

```
(* OCaml *)
let f l = List.fold_right (fun x acc -> "(" ^
    (string_of_int x) ^ "+" ^ acc ^ ")") l "0"
```

What are the values of the following expressions?

```
f [] = ?
f [1] = ?
f [1; 2] = ?
```

Please select all following choices that apply.

Choice A:

```
f [] = "0"
f [1] = "1"
f [1; 2] = "3"
```

Choice B:

```
f [] = "0"
f [1] = "(1+0)"
f [1; 2] = "(1+(2+0))"
```

5.7.6 Quiz 6

Assume we have the following functions:

`zipWith`

```
let rec zipWith f l1 l2 = match l1, l2 with
```

The Art of Functional Programming

5 COMMON COMPUTATION PATTERNS

```
2        | [], _ -> []
3        | _, [] -> []
4        | x :: xs, y :: ys
            -> f x y ::
            zipWith f xs ys
```

all

```
1  let all l = List.fold_right (&&) l true
```

Using these functions, we define the following function:

```
1  let f l = match l with
2           | [] -> true
3           | hd :: tl -> all (zipWith (=) l (
              List.tl l))
```

What does f do?

Please select all following choices that apply.

Choice A: It returns `true` if all elements of a list are different and `false` otherwise.

Choice B: It returns `true` if all elements of a list are equals and `false` otherwise.

5.7.7 Quiz 7

The following algebraic datatype defines natural numbers:

```
1  (* OCaml *)
2  type nat = Zero | Succ of nat
```

Moreover, the following function implements `fold` on nat:

5 COMMON COMPUTATION PATTERNS

```ocaml
(* OCaml *)
let rec fold_nat f init n = match n with
                            | Zero -> init
                            | Succ m -> f (
                               fold_nat f
                               init m)
```

We use `fold_nat` to define the following function:

```ocaml
(* OCaml *)
let f = fold_nat ((^) "-") ""
```

What are the values of the following expressions?

```
f Zero = ?
f (Succ Zero) = ?
f (Succ (Succ Zero)) = ?
```

Please select all following choices that apply.

Choice A:

```
f Zero = ""
f (Succ Zero) = "(-)"
f (Succ (Succ Zero)) = "(--)"
```

Choice B:

```
f Zero = ""
f (Succ Zero) = "-"
f (Succ (Succ Zero)) = "--"
```

5.7.8 Quiz 8

Haskell defines the following *typeclass* called `Functor`:

5 COMMON COMPUTATION PATTERNS

```haskell
-- Haskell
class Functor f where
    fmap :: (a -> b) -> f a -> f b
    (<$) :: a -> f b -> f a
```

Here f represents some *type*.

The fmap function looks quite familiar, doesn't it? What does fmap capture?

Please select all following choices that apply.

Choice A: It captures the general type of map on any container, domain, or context denoted by f.

Choice B: It captures a binary function denoted by f.

5.8 Answers to Quiz on Common Computation Patterns

5.8.1 Quiz 1

Choice B is correct. Here, (+) 1 is a function that increases an input by 1. We use List.map to apply that increment function to the elements of the list [1; 2; 3].

5.8.2 Quiz 2

Choice B is correct. The zipWith function takes as input a binary function f and two lists l1 and l2. It produces a new list whose elements result from applying f to l1 and l2 elements.

5 COMMON COMPUTATION PATTERNS

5.8.3 Quiz 3

Choice A is correct. The OCaml's built-in function `fst` returns the first component of a pair. Here, we use `List.map` to extract the x coordinates of `points`.

5.8.4 Quiz 4

Choice A is correct. This quiz demonstrates that `fold` is a highly general abstraction. Even `filter` is just a particular case of `fold`.

5.8.5 Quiz 5

Choice B is correct. This quiz is another demonstration of how the function is called `fold_right`. Notice the sum associates to the right.

5.8.6 Quiz 6

Choice B is correct.

For example,

```
1  f [] = true
2  f [1] = true
3  f [1; 1] = true
4  f [1; 2] = true
```

5 COMMON COMPUTATION PATTERNS

5.8.7 Quiz 7

Choice B is correct. The function `f` converts a `nat` into a string representation. If `nat` represents an integer number n, the resulting string is --- ... --- (n times -).

5.8.8 Quiz 8

Choice A is correct. `Functor` in Haskell captures a type that can be mapped over.

6 Dataflow Programming with Functions

6.1 List-based Dataflow Programming

6.1.1 Dataflow programming paradigm

Dataflow programming is a programming paradigm in which we model programs as directed graphs consisting of nodes and directed edges connecting the nodes. A node represents an operation that accepts inputs and produces output. A directed edge from node A to node B sends A's output as B's input. To illustrate, let's use an example of arithmetic calculation from Bert Sutherland's Ph.D. thesis titled *"The on-line graphical specification of computer procedures,"* which pioneered dataflow programming.

6 DATAFLOW PROGRAMMING WITH FUNCTIONS

Textual representation

$Z = A \cdot B + C$
$W = Z + 4$
$Y = Z^2 - (3 \cdot Z + B)$

Graphical representation

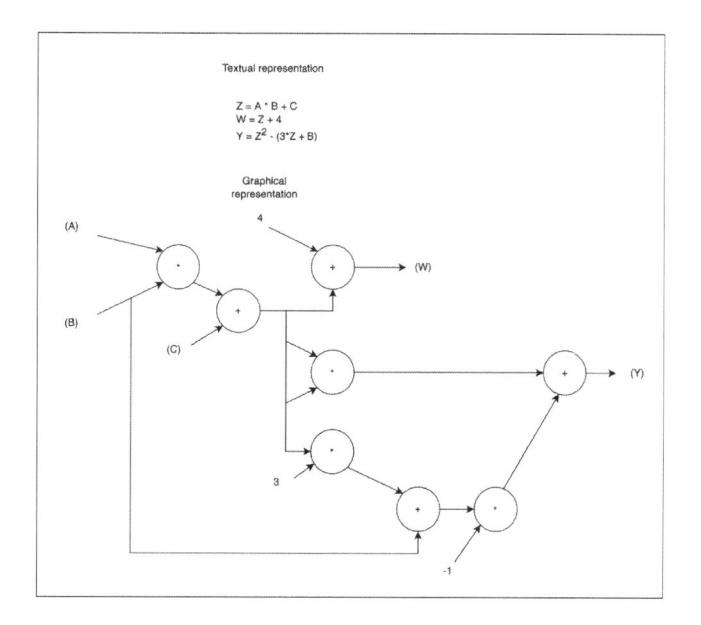

Figure 64: Arithmetic calculation as a dataflow program

Compared to the textual representation, the graphical one follows the dataflow programming style by emphasizing how the data flows from one operation to the other. This has several advantages. First, the dataflow-oriented program describes how the program is made up of smaller building blocks and, therefore, relatively easy to understand. Second, the dataflow version enables parallel execution without any extra effort from the programmer. The executor of the dataflow program can automatically determine which operations can be run in parallel based on the data dependencies between them. In our example, W and Y can be calculated simultaneously because they don't depend on each other.

6 DATAFLOW PROGRAMMING WITH FUNCTIONS

This paradigm generally encourages the creation of a library of general-purpose components. This library can be used to construct programs, usually in the form of visual programming. When we mix and match existing components to build programs, we save tons of development time and effort compared to writing and implementing them from scratch. Moreover, the building blocks can be combined to solve problems not even envisioned by their creators.

Dataflow programming is commonly employed by embedded software engineers who develop control systems, such as cruise control for cars. A functional programming language allows us to program in the dataflow-oriented style and reap all its benefits.

6.1.2 Functions as dataflow components

In functional programming languages, functions are pure. This means that they always return the same output for the same input, and their application has no side effects. Due to these properties, functions in the functional paradigm behave similarly to dataflow components – they also accept input and produce output without causing any side effects. Note that if a set of functions agree on a common input/output data format, we can compose them in the dataflow style.

Let's consider three functions – `map`, `filter`, and `fold`. We can view those functions as dataflow components. In particular, map acts as a dataflow component that maps each element of the input signal to a new value in the output signal. It is a general-purpose

6 DATAFLOW PROGRAMMING WITH FUNCTIONS

component usable for many use cases because it allows us to configure the mapping function `f` to whatever we want.

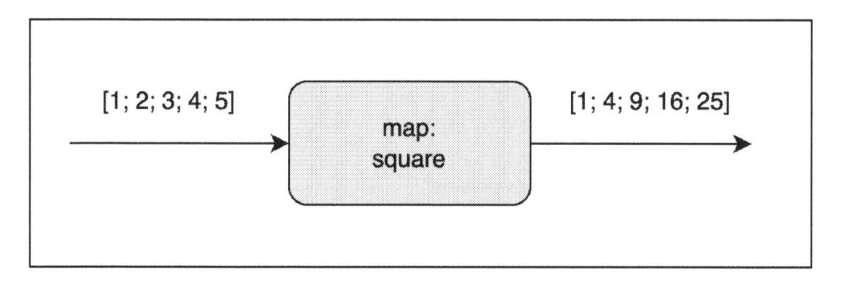

Figure 65: Map as a dataflow component

The `filter` component allows those elements of the input signal to pass through only if they satisfy a predicate. It is also a highly reusable component because it enables us to configure the predicate to meet our use case.

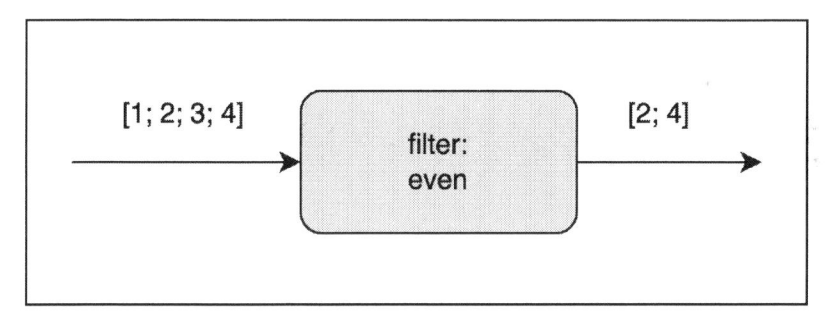

Figure 66: 'filter' as a dataflow component

We can also view `fold`, which accumulates an input signal into a value, as a dataflow component. We can configure its initial value and an accumulation function.

6 DATAFLOW PROGRAMMING WITH FUNCTIONS

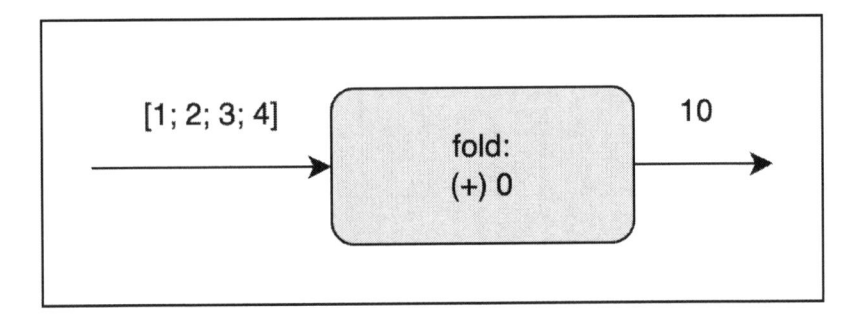

Figure 67: 'fold' as a dataflow component

All these functions use lists as a common interface. For instance, `map` and `filter` accept a list as input and return a list as output. The `fold` function takes a list as an argument and returns an aggregated value. This allows us to do dataflow programming by constructing programs as graphs whose nodes are list processing functions, such as `map`, `filter`, and `fold`.

To illustrate, assume we want to implement a `sum_even_squares` function that calculates the sum of squares of all even numbers within an interval a and b. For example, $sum\_even\_squares\ 1\ 4 = 2^2 + 4^2 = 20$

Of course, we can quickly write a recursive function to do this, as shown below:

```
(* OCaml *)
let even x = x mod 2 = 0
let square x = x * x

let rec sum_even_squares a b =
    if a > b then 0 else
```

6 DATAFLOW PROGRAMMING WITH FUNCTIONS

```
      let x = if even a then square a else 0 in x
        + sum_even_squares (a + 1) b

sum_even_squares 1 4
(* Result: 20 *)
```

However, there is no need to implement `sum_even_squares` from scratch. Instead, it is far more efficient to compose a solution by reusing the existing components – `map`, `filter`, and `fold`. The key is to recognize that we can define `sum_even_squares` as a dataflow program that processes the data in the following stages:

- Enumerate integers between a and b as a list.
- Filter the list and only keep even numbers.
- Map each element to its square.
- Fold the list elements using +, starting with 0 to accumulate to sum.

The following diagram visualizes this program:

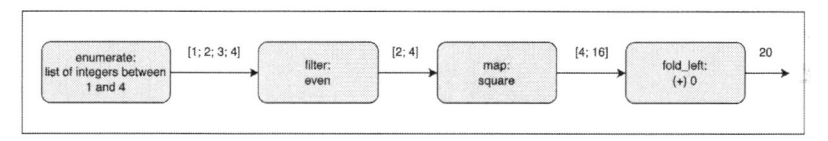

Figure 68: 'sum_even_squares' as a dataflow diagram

Looking at the diagram, it becomes clear that the only thing we need to do is enumerate integers within an interval of [a, b]. We can use `filter`, `map`, and `fold` to define all the other stages.

We can define the following function to enumerate integers between a and b as a list:

6 DATAFLOW PROGRAMMING WITH FUNCTIONS

```ocaml
(* OCaml *)
let rec enumerate_integers a b = if a > b then
    [] else a :: enumerate_integers (a + 1) b

enumerate_integers 1 4
(* Result [1; 2; 3; 4] *)
```

Next, we translate the dataflow diagram for `sum_even_squares` into OCaml code, as shown below:

```ocaml
(* OCaml *)
let sum_even_squares a b = List.fold_left (+)
    0 (List.map square (List.filter even (
    enumerate_integers a b)))

sum_even_squares 1 4
(* Result: 20 *)
```

There is one thing that is not optimal. While the dataflow diagram shows the processing stages from left to right, the textual version has a reversed order. We can use OCaml's pipe operator |> to change this. It allows us to pass an argument to a function from left to right. This operator is defined below:

```
x |> f = f x
```

We can use this operator to create an improved version of `sum_even_squares`.

```ocaml
(* OCaml *)
let sum_even_squares a b = enumerate_integers
    a b |> List.filter even |> List.map square
    |> List.fold_left (+) 0
```

6 DATAFLOW PROGRAMMING WITH FUNCTIONS

This version looks closer to the dataflow diagram above because it emphasizes that the data flows from left to right.

As another example, let's say we want to write another function called `sum_tree_even_squares`. This function sums up the squares of all even nodes in a binary tree represented by the following algebraic data type:

```
(* OCaml *)
type 'a bin_tree =
        | Leaf
        | Node of 'a bin_tree * 'a * 'a
          bin_tree
```

Adopting the dataflow programming paradigm, we can construct the following dataflow diagram to solve the program:

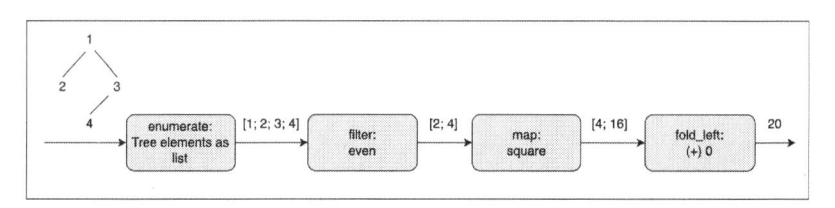

Figure 69: 'sum_tree_even_squares' as a dataflow program

Except for the first stage, this looks exactly like `sum_even_squares` for the lists above. We have to enumerate all elements in a tree as a list. We can do that by folding over the tree, as shown below:

```
(* OCaml *)
let enumerate_tree_elements l = fold_tree (fun
       l x r -> x :: l @ r) [] l
```

6 DATAFLOW PROGRAMMING WITH FUNCTIONS

Here `fold_tree` folds a binary tree.

```ocaml
(* OCaml *)
let rec fold_tree f init t =
    match t with
    | Leaf -> init
    | Node (l, x, r) -> f (fold_tree f init l)
        x (fold_tree f init r)
```

Next, we connect the components to formulate a function that calculates the sum of squares of even nodes.

```ocaml
(* OCaml *)
let sum_tree_even_squares t =
    enumerate_tree_elements t |> List.filter
    even |> List.map square |> List.fold_left
    (+) 0
```

The functions `map` and `fold` accept a single list as input. Therefore, we can view them as components of a single input signal through the lens of dataflow programming. For functions with several input lists, we can view them as dataflow components that accept multiple input signals. For example, `zipWith` acts as a component that produces a signal from two input signals.

6 DATAFLOW PROGRAMMING WITH FUNCTIONS

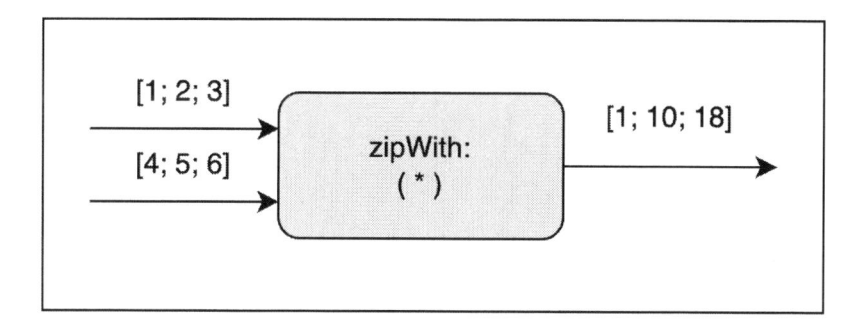

Figure 70: 'zipWith' as a dataflow component

Let's build a dataflow program using `zipWith`. This program will count the prime numbers less than or equal to n in the form of a list of strings. For instance, if n is 6, the output should be `["Prime at 1 is 2"; "Prime at 2 is 3", "Prime at 3 is 5"]`.

The following dataflow diagram is one way to solve this problem:

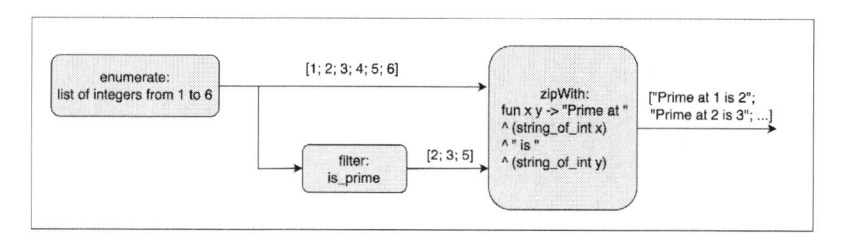

Figure 71: Dataflow program to count prime numbers

We can translate the diagram into OCaml code as follows.

```
(* OCaml *)
let count_primes n =
    let l = enumerate_integers 1 n in
```

6 DATAFLOW PROGRAMMING WITH FUNCTIONS

```
4     zipWith (fun x y -> "Prime at " ^ (
        string_of_int x) ^ " is " ^ (
        string_of_int y)) l (List.filter
        is_prime l)
5
6   count_primes 6
7   (* Result: ["Prime at 1 is 2"; "Prime at 2 is
        3"; "Prime at 3 is 5"] *)
```

6.1.3 Rule of composition

In his wonderful book, *The Art of Unix Programming*, Eric Steven Raymond discusses the Unix philosophy – A set of reflections about software development hard-earned from the experiences of developing the highly successful Unix operating system.

One essential aspect of the Unix philosophy is what Raymond called the **rule of composition**. It states that we should favor small, independent programs that do one thing and do it well. Moreover, we should aim to build programs whose inputs and outputs are plain text streams rather than binary data. The plain text serves as a universal interface to exchange information between programs. Thanks to this, the output of one program can be sent as input of another program via a pipe operator written as vertical bar, |.

For example, a Unix operating system usually provides the following programs:

- `cat`: This creates files or views the content of a file.
- `head`: This prints the first lines of the input. For instance, `head -5` prints the first 5 lines.

6 DATAFLOW PROGRAMMING WITH FUNCTIONS

- `tail`: This prints the last lines of the input. For instance, `tail -5` prints the last 5 lines.

On a Unix or macOS system, the `/usr/share/dict/words` file is an English dictionary that contains a list of words, each on a new line.

```
1   A
2   a
3   aa
4   aal
5   aalii
6   aam
7   Aani
8   aardvark
9   aardwolf
10  Aaron
11  Aaronic
12  ...
```

How can we print the 5th word of the dictionary? Instead of implementing a new program from scratch, we can compose the existing programs `cat`, `head` and `tail` to achieve that functionality. We use the following command to do that:

```
1   cat /usr/share/dict/words | head -5 | tail -1
2   aalii
```

The following diagram shows how the programs are connected:

6 DATAFLOW PROGRAMMING WITH FUNCTIONS

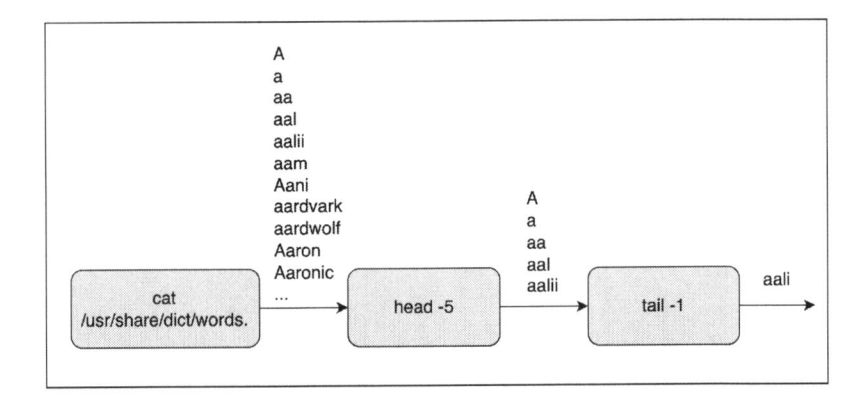

Figure 72: Compose Unix programs

Essentially, cat reads the dictionary's content, which is sent to head via the pipe operator, |. The head -10 program returns the first 5 lines. For these, the tail -1 program picks the last line, which is the 5th word.

We have followed the rule of composition throughout this section. In particular, the functions – map, filter, fold, and zipWith – are small, independent programs that can do one thing well. For instance, map is good at transforming elements, while fold is ideal for aggregating data. The universal interface that allows these programs to be composable is list. The OCaml's pipe operator, |>, is conceptually similar to the Unix pipe operator, |. The rule of composition is a part of what makes the Unix operating system so successful. We can harness that same power with functional programming.

6 DATAFLOW PROGRAMMING WITH FUNCTIONS

6.2 Stream-based Dataflow Programming

6.2.1 Limitations of list-based dataflow programming

The functional paradigm allows us to formulate programs in the dataflow style by composing function lists, such as `map`, `filter`, and `fold`. Unfortunately, list-based dataflow programming in OCaml has a severe limitation – lists are finite.

To illustrate, suppose we implement a function that returns the first prime number greater than or equal to a given n. The function is named `first_prime_greater_equal`. We can attempt to formulate a dataflow program to solve this problem with the following steps:

- Enumerate integers greater than or equal n
- Filter the list, keeping only prime numbers
- Take the head of the resulting list

In other words, we attempt to formulate the following dataflow diagram:

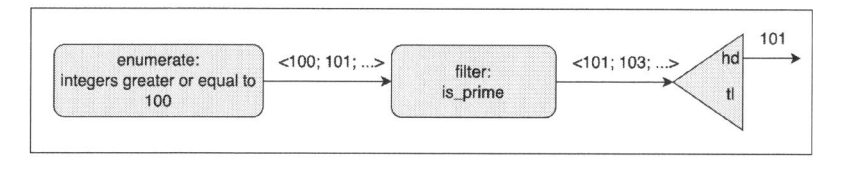

Figure 73: Attempt to formulate 'first_prime_greater_equal' as a dataflow program

To differentiate an infinite list from a finite one, we will write infinitely many elements in triangle brackets, e.g., <100; 101; 102; ...>.

Unfortunately, as elegant as the dataflow diagram is, we can not formulate it. The `enumerate` and `filter` components need to work with signals of infinitely many elements. However, OCaml lists can only hold a finite number of elements. To see why, let's try to define a list of infinite natural numbers: <0; 1; 2; ...> with the following recursive function:

```
(* OCaml *)
let rec naturals_from n = n :: naturals_from (
    n + 1)
```

We apply that function to 0 to obtain the sequence of naturals (0, 1, 2,...).

```
(* OCaml *)
let naturals = naturals_from 0
```

If we run the code above, we'll see a stack overflow exception. This is because when we try to apply `naturals_from` 0, it calls `naturals_from` 1, which calls `naturals_from` 2, and so forth. This continues until the stack limit is reached. In other words, because OCaml is a strict language, the `hd :: tl` list constructor always evaluates the two arguments, `hd` and `tl`, regardless of whether their values are needed or not.

To circumvent the problem of infinite elements, we can define a `first_prime_between` function that returns the first prime number between a and b. Since the [a, b] range is finite, we can formulate a list-based dataflow program to solve this problem.

6 DATAFLOW PROGRAMMING WITH FUNCTIONS

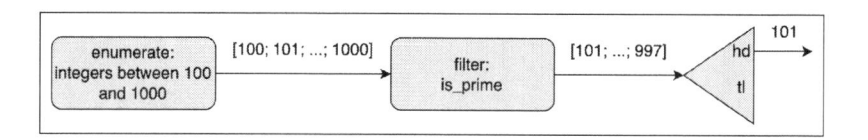

Figure 74: 'first_prime_between' as list-based dataflow diagram

We can implement `first_prime_between` in OCaml as follows.

```
(* OCaml *)
let first_prime_between a b =
    enumerate_integers a b |> List.filter
    is_prime |> List.hd

first_prime_between 100 1000
(* Result: 101 *)
```

Although this function works, it's incredibly inefficient. It enumerates all integers from 100 to 1000, and `filter` checks every single number to see if it's prime or not. It would be much more efficient to incrementally check whether a candidate is a prime number starting from a (100 in this example). Once a prime number is found, the execution stops.

In an imperative programming language like Java, we can implement this incremental computation with a loop and `break` or `return`.

```
// Java
int firstPrimeBetween(int a, int b) {
    int candidate = a;
    while (candidate <= b) {
        if (isPrime(candidate)) {
            return candidate;
```

6 DATAFLOW PROGRAMMING WITH FUNCTIONS

```
7          }
8          candidate++;
9        }
10       return -1;
11   }
```

However, this imperative version lacks the clarity and composability of the dataflow-oriented program above.

Ideally, we want to achieve the best of both of these versions. In other words, we want to do the following:

- Compose components to construct programs in the dataflow style as we do with lists.
- Create signals can contain an infinite number of elements.
- Benefit from the efficiency of incremental computation.

We can do this with the help of the stream data structure. But before we can define a stream type, let's discuss how to delay an evaluation.

6.2.2 Delay evaluation

Since functions are first-class values in OCaml, they are easy to delay. We simply wrap the function inside another function without an argument. To illustrate, suppose we've defined the following `fib` function calculating the `n-th` Fibonacci:

```
1  (* OCaml *)
2  let rec fib n = if n <= 2 then 1 else fib (n
       -1) + fib (n-2)
3
```

6 DATAFLOW PROGRAMMING WITH FUNCTIONS

```
4  fib 40
5  (* Result: 102334155 *)
```

If we run the code above, we'll notice that it takes a while for the `fib 40` call to complete before the result is shown. We delay the evaluation of `fib40`, when we wrapped it inside a function without argument.

```
1  (* OCaml *)
2  let delayed_fib40 = fun () -> fib 40
```

A function without an argument formed to delay an evaluation like `delayed_fib40` is called a thunk. When we need the value of `fib 40`, we apply the `delayed_fib40` thunk to no argument.

```
1  (* OCaml *)
2  delayed_fib40 ()
3
4  (* Result: 102334155 *)
```

OCaml provides a built-in keyword called `lazy` that we can use to delay the evaluation of an expression, like the `fib 40` calculation, as shown below:

```
1  (* OCaml *)
2  let delayed_fib40 = lazy (fib 40)
```

The type of `delayed_fib40` is int `lazy_t`, which indicates that `delayed_fib40` is a delayed evaluation that produces an integer when evaluated. OCaml also provides a function called `Lazy.force` that forces an expression delayed by `lazy` to evaluate.

Let's try out `lazy` and `Lazy.force` in the code snippet below.

The Art of Functional Programming

6 DATAFLOW PROGRAMMING WITH FUNCTIONS

```ocaml
(* OCaml *)
let rec fib n = if n <= 2 then 1 else fib (n
    -1) + fib (n-2)

let delayed_fib40 = lazy (fib 40)

Lazy.force delayed_fib40
(* Result: 102334155*)
```

It's worth mentioning that OCaml's implementation of `lazy` and `Lazy.force` accommodates the memoization. Once a delayed evaluation is forced to evaluate, its result is cached/memoized. The cached result is returned for future calls, and no expensive calculation incurs. In our example, the first time we call `Lazy.force delayed_fib40`, the evaluation takes a while to complete. This is because `fib 40` is quite an expensive call. However, if we force `delayed_fib40` to evaluate the second time, it returns the results instantaneously.

6.2.3 Stream is a delayed list

We can define a stream data structure as a delayed list where the tail is a delayed evaluation. Additionally, we might avoid an empty stream `Nil`. This is because streams can have infinite elements, which leads to the following definition in OCaml:

```ocaml
(* OCaml *)
type 'a stream = Cons of 'a * 'a stream Lazy.t
```

We can think of a stream as a pair whose first element is available. The second element is a delayed evaluation that promises to pro-

6 DATAFLOW PROGRAMMING WITH FUNCTIONS

duce the next stream. The head of this stream contains the second element and its tail is yet another delayed evaluation. And so on and so forth.

Let's define two selectors, `stream_hd` (head) and `stream_tl` (tail), to extract the head and tail from a stream:

```ocaml
(* OCaml *)
let stream_hd (Cons (h, _)) = h
let stream_tl (Cons (_, t)) = Lazy.force t
```

The `stream_hd` function is straightforward – it simply returns the head of the stream. However, `stream_tl` is a more interesting function because it forces the tail to evaluate using `Lazy.force`. The `stream_hd` and `stream_tl` functions make up a dataflow component to extract elements out of a signal.

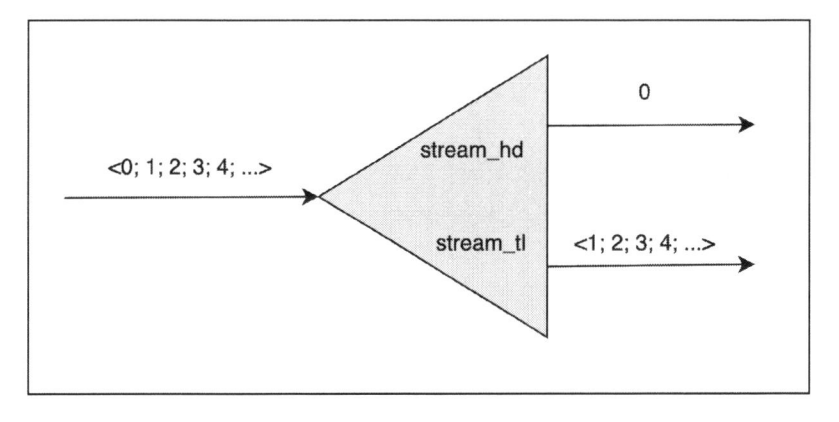

Figure 75: Signal extractor as a dataflow component

We can use the `stream` data structure to formulate a `naturals_from` function that enumerates a sequence of an infinite number of

6 DATAFLOW PROGRAMMING WITH FUNCTIONS

naturals starting from `n`.

```
(* OCaml *)
let rec naturals_from n = Cons (n, lazy (
    naturals_from (n+1)))
```

The stack overflow problem does not occur this time. That is because we use `lazy` to delay the evaluation of `naturals_from (n+1)`. We can apply `naturals_from` to 0 to obtain the infinite sequence of all natural numbers.

```
(* OCaml *)
let naturals = naturals_from 0
```

The stream makes the first natural number 0 available at its head. The tail is a delayed evaluation. When evaluated, it produces a stream that contains the second natural number, 1, and another delayed evaluation, and so on and so forth.

There is a challenge when working with streams. We can't see beyond its first element because the tail is not evaluated yet. To inspect the stream elements, we can define a `stream_take` function to return a list of the first n elements of the stream.

```
(* OCaml *)
let rec stream_take n s =
    if n <= 0 then [] else stream_hd s ::
        stream_take (n-1) (stream_tl s)

stream_take 10 naturals
(* Result: [0; 1; 2; 3; 4; 5; 6; 7; 8; 9] *)
```

Note that the `stream_take` function forces the stream to produce as many elements as needed. In the case of `stream_take 10`

6 DATAFLOW PROGRAMMING WITH FUNCTIONS

naturals, the stream produces precisely 10 elements.

6.2.4 Higher-order functions on streams

Similar to lists, we can define reusable higher-order functions on streams.

stream_map

Analogous to how the map function works for lists, we can define a higher-order function stream_map. This function applies a mapping to each element of an input stream.

```
1  (* OCaml *)
2  let rec stream_map f s = Cons (f (stream_hd s)
     , lazy (stream_map f (stream_tl s)))
```

The exciting part here is that we use lazy to delay the evaluation of the stream_map function's call to the stream's tail.

We can use stream_map to construct a stream of square numbers. This stream, square_naturals, produces a sequence of square numbers.

```
1  (* OCaml *)
2  let square_naturals = stream_map (fun x -> x *
     x) naturals
3
4  stream_take 10 square_naturals
5  (* Result: [0; 1; 4; 9; 16; 25; 36; 49; 64;
     81] *)
```

We can view stream_map as a dataflow component that maps the input signal to the output signal.

6 DATAFLOW PROGRAMMING WITH FUNCTIONS

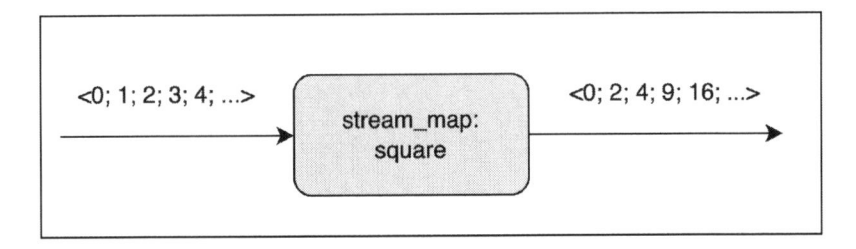

Figure 76: 'stream_map' as a dataflow component

The crucial difference between `stream_map` and `List.map` is that the input and output signals of `stream_map` might have infinite elements. On the contrary, `List.map` only works with signals of finite elements.

stream_filter

We can also define a higher-order function `stream_filter`. This function produces a new stream from an input stream by allowing only the elements that satisfy the predicate to pass through.

```ocaml
(* OCaml *)
let rec stream_filter p s =
    if p (stream_hd s) then Cons (stream_hd s,
        lazy (stream_filter p (stream_tl s)))
    else stream_filter p (stream_tl s)
```

We can formulate a stream of even numbers by piping the natural numbers into a `stream_filter` function, which only allows even numbers to pass through.

```ocaml
(* OCaml *)
let evens = stream_filter (fun x -> x mod 2 =
    0) naturals
```

6 DATAFLOW PROGRAMMING WITH FUNCTIONS

```
3
4  stream_take 10 evens
5  (* Result: [0; 2; 4; 6; 8; 10; 12; 14; 16; 18]
   *)
```

We can view `stream_filter` through the dataflow-oriented lens, as shown below:

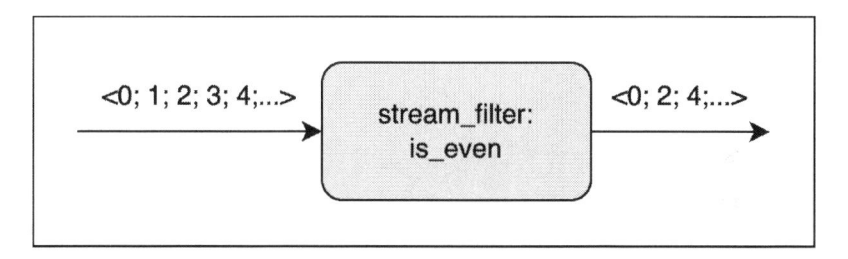

Figure 77: 'stream_filter' as a dataflow component

The `stream_filter` function will keep asking the input stream for a new element that satisfies the predicate until it finds one. If no such element exists, `stream_filter` never returns.

Combining two streams with `stream_zipWith`

We can define higher-order functions that combine multiple streams. For instance, the following `stream_zipWith` function is the stream version of `zipWith`. This function takes as arguments a binary function f and two input streams. It produces a new stream whose elements result from applying f to the elements of the input streams.

```
1  (* OCaml *)
2  let rec stream_zipWith f s1 s2 =
```

6 DATAFLOW PROGRAMMING WITH FUNCTIONS

```
3           Cons (f (stream_hd s1) (stream_hd s2),
            lazy (stream_zipWith f (stream_tl s1
            ) (stream_tl s2)))
```

For example, `stream_zipWith ( * )` accepts two streams and produces a new stream of corresponding multiplications. We can use it to create a stream of squares of natural numbers.

```
1  (* OCaml *)
2  let square_naturals = stream_zipWith ( * )
      naturals naturals
3
4  stream_take 10 square_naturals
5  (* Result: [0; 1; 4; 9; 16; 25; 36; 49; 64;
      81] *)
```

We can view `stream_zipWith` as a dataflow component, as shown below:

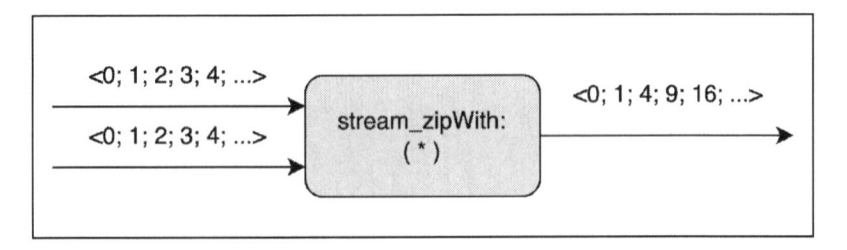

Figure 78: 'stream_zipWith' as a dataflow component

An exciting part of `stream_zipWith` is that it transparently supports synchronization. The function waits until both input streams can provide elements. Next, it applies the function to produce an element for the resulting sequence.

6   DATAFLOW PROGRAMMING WITH FUNCTIONS

6.2.5 Stream-based dataflow programming

We can compose `stream_hd`, `stream_tl`, `stream_map`, and `stream_filter` in the dataflow style to construct programs. Streams serve as the common interface to connect these functions. Stream-based dataflow programming has all the beauty and elegance of list-based dataflow programming, with two added advantages. First, we can formulate dataflow programs that deal with signals of an infinite number of elements. Second, since streams allow computations to be triggered on-demand, we can fully benefit from the efficiency of incremental computation.

Let's use `stream` to formulate the `first_prime_greater_equal n` function which returns the first prime number greater than or equal to n.

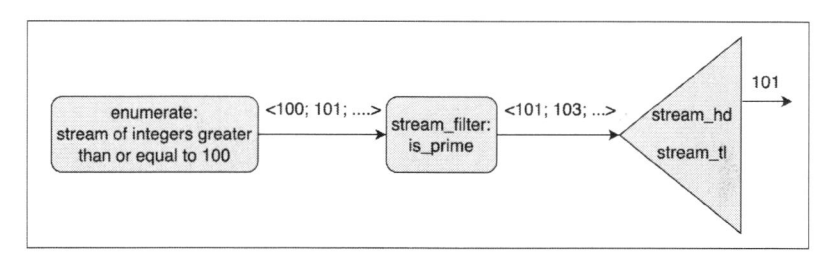

Figure 79: 'first_prime_greater_equal' as a stream-based dataflow diagram

We convert the above dataflow diagram into OCaml in the code below:

```
(* OCaml *)
```

6 DATAFLOW PROGRAMMING WITH FUNCTIONS

```
2  let first_prime_greater_equal n = stream_hd (
       stream_filter is_prime (naturals_from n))
3
4  first_prime_greater_equal 100
5  (* Result: 101 *)
```

Optionally, we can use the OCaml pipe operator |> to make the flow from left to right like in the diagram.

```
1  (* OCaml *)
2  let first_prime_greater_equal n =
       naturals_from n |> stream_filter is_prime
       |> stream_hd
```

Thanks to streams, it is possible to define an enumerator that generates infinitely many natural streams. Furthermore, the `first_prime_greater_equal` function searches incrementally for the first prime number. This means that the stream of natural numbers keeps producing candidates as long as it is not a prime number. Once a prime number is found as the filter requires, the stream stops producing further candidates.

6.2.6 Infinite lists in non-strict languages

OCaml lists are finite because OCaml is a strict language. Whenever OCaml evaluates a list of a form `hd :: tl`, it always evaluates both `hd` and `tl`. This prevents the lists from delaying the tail, and as a result, from representing infinite sequences.

However, in a non-strict language, notably Haskell, lists can be infinite. The following Haskell code snippet illustrates this.

6 DATAFLOW PROGRAMMING WITH FUNCTIONS

```haskell
-- Haskell
naturals_from n = n : naturals_from (n+1)
naturals = naturals_from 0

take 10 naturals
-- Result: [0,1,2,3,4,5,6,7,8,9]
```

When we run the code above, it does not throw a no stack overflow exception like the OCaml version. This is because `naturals_from 0` evaluates to `0 : naturals 1`, but Haskell does not evaluate `naturals 1` because its value is not needed yet. This has the same effect as when we use the `lazy` keyword to delay the evaluation.

Strict or non-strict is a language design decision that has pros and cons either way. The advantage of non-strict in languages such as Haskell is that a list can act as a stream. However, strict semantics makes it harder to reason about space and time. On the other hand, non-strictness can result in undesirable side effects.

The main takeaway from this section is that streams and stream functions allow us to do stream-based dataflow programming with many benefits. These benefits include the following:

- The programs are constructed by composing components.
- The signals flowing through components can have an infinite number of elements.
- The computation is done incrementally.

6.3 Programming Challenges

Let's solve coding challenges to practice dataflow programming with functions.

6.3.1 Challenge 1: Area of the largest circle

The following algebraic datatype represents a geometric shape. For our purposes here, we'll only consider circles and rectangles.

```ocaml
(* OCaml *)
type shape = Circle of float
           | Rectangle of float * float
```

The following function calculates the area of a shape:

```ocaml
(* OCaml *)
let rec area s = match s with
                 | Circle r -> 3.14 *. r *. r
                 | Rectangle (w, h) -> w *. h
```

Write an OCaml function, `max_circle`, that takes as an input a list of shapes and returns the area of the largest circle in the list.

For example:

```ocaml
(* OCaml *)
max_circle [] = 0.
max_circle [Circle 1.; Rectangle (1., 2.);
    Circle 2.; Rectangle (2., 3.)] = 12.56
```

In this challenge, try to think of how you could define a dataflow diagram to solve the problem.

6 DATAFLOW PROGRAMMING WITH FUNCTIONS

6.3.2 Challenge 2: Merge two streams

Write an OCaml function `stream_merge` that can merge two streams into one by taking elements alternatively.

For example:

```
(* OCaml *)
stream_take 10 (stream_merge evens odds) = [0;
    1; 2; 3; 4; 5; 6; 7; 8; 9]
stream_take 10 (stream_merge odds evens) = [1;
    0; 3; 2; 5; 4; 7; 6; 9; 8]
```

Where `odds` and `evens` are streams of odd and even natural numbers, respectively.

```
(* OCaml *)
evens = <0; 2; 4; 6; 8;...>
odds = <1; 3; 5; 7; 9;...>
```

6.3.3 Challenge 3: Stream of Fibonacci numbers

Suppose we have a stream of Fibonacci numbers, <1; 1; 2; 3; 5; 8; ...>. If we zip it with its tail, <1; 2; 3; 5; 8; 13; ...>, using the addition function (+), we get the <2; 3; 5; 8; 13; ...> stream. This obtained stream is the tail of the tail of our original stream of Fibonacci.

Write a stream called `fibs` in OCaml that contains all Fibonacci numbers based on the observation above.

6 DATAFLOW PROGRAMMING WITH FUNCTIONS

6.4 Solutions to Programming Challenges

6.4.1 Challenge 1: Area of the largest circle

We can formulate `max_circle` as a dataflow program consisting of the following phases:

- Filter the list of shapes, keeping only circles
- Map each circle to its area
- Fold the list using `max` starting with `0.0` to calculate the maximal area, where `max` returns the maximum of two given numbers

Recall that we can use the OCaml pipe operator, `|>`, to make the data flow from left to right.

The following is a possible implementation of the dataflow program above in OCaml.

```
(* OCaml *)
let max_circle l = l |> List.filter is_circle
     |> List.map area |> List.fold_left max 0.
```

6.4.2 Challenge 2: Merge two streams

The `merge` stream consists of the first element of the first input stream and the delayed evaluation of the recursive call, which merges the second input stream with the tail of the first one.

```
(* OCaml *)
```

6 DATAFLOW PROGRAMMING WITH FUNCTIONS

```
2 let rec stream_merge (Cons (x, xs)) s2 = Cons
      (x, lazy (stream_merge s2 (Lazy.force xs))
      )
```

6.4.3 Challenge 3: Stream of Fibonacci numbers

We can implement `fibs` in OCaml as follows:

```
1 (* OCaml *)
2 let rec fibs = Cons (1, lazy (Cons (2, lazy (
      stream_zipWith (+) fibs (stream_tl fibs)))
      ))
```

6.5 Quiz on Dataflow Programming with Functions

Let's test your understanding of dataflow programming with functions.

6.5.1 Quiz 1

What are the key ideas of Unix philosophy's rule of composition?

Please select all following choices that apply.

Choice A: We should favor big programs that contain as many features as possible. This way, less time is wasted on developing many programs.

Choice B: We should favor small, independent programs that do one thing and do it well.

6 DATAFLOW PROGRAMMING WITH FUNCTIONS

Choice C: Programs should use plain text for input and output.

Choice D: Programs should use binary format for input and output.

6.5.2 Quiz 2

Why can we build dataflow programs with functions in the functional paradigm?

Please select all following choices that apply.

Choice A: Functions have no side effects in the functional paradigm.

Choice B: We can draw boxes and lines in a functional paradigm.

Choice C: Various functions can be connected to each other by relying on a shared interface like lists or streams.

6.5.3 Quiz 3

Given the square function:

```
(* OCaml *)
let square x = x * x
```

What is the result of the following OCaml expression?

```
(* OCaml *)
2 |> square
```

Please select all following choices that apply.

6 DATAFLOW PROGRAMMING WITH FUNCTIONS

Choice A: 2

Choice B: 4

6.5.4 Quiz 4

What is the value of the following OCaml code that implements a dataflow program?

```
(* OCaml *)
[0; 1; 2] |> List.map (fun x -> x > 0) |> List
    .fold_left (&&) true
```

Please select all following choices that apply.

Choice A: 0

Choice B: true

Choice C: false

6.5.5 Quiz 5

What are some of the key benefits of using streams?

Please select all following choices that apply.

Choice A: Streams make it easy to represent a finite sequence of data.

Choice B: Streams allow us to model infinite sequences of data.

Choice C: Streams allow us to benefit from incremental computation since data is calculated on demand.

6 DATAFLOW PROGRAMMING WITH FUNCTIONS

6.5.6 Quiz 6

What is the result of the following OCaml expression?

```
1  (* OCaml *)
2  [1; 2; 3; 4] |> List.filter ((<=) 3) |> List.
       map (( * ) 2) |> List.fold_left (+) 0
```

Please select all following choices that apply.

Choice A: 10

Choice A: 20

Choice A: 40

6.5.7 Quiz 7

What is the value of the following OCaml expression?

```
1  (* OCaml *)
2  lazy (1/0)
```

Please select all following choices that apply.

Choice A: It throws a `Division by zero` exception.

Choice A: It is a delayed evaluation of type `lazy_t`.

Choice C: 1

6.5.8 Quiz 8

Given the following OCaml expression

6 DATAFLOW PROGRAMMING WITH FUNCTIONS

```
(* OCaml *)
let expr = lazy (1/0)
```

What is the value of the following OCaml expression?

```
(* OCaml *)
Lazy.force expr
```

Please select all following choices that apply.

Choice A: It throws a `Division by zero` exception.

Choice A: 1

Choice C: It is a delayed evaluation.

6.6 Answers to Quiz on Dataflow Programming with Functions

6.6.1 Quiz 1

Choice B and C is correct. Small, independent programs can do one thing well and are easier to compose. Moreover, plain text acts as a shared interface to connect various programs with each other to solve problems that individual programs cannot.

6.6.2 Quiz 2

Choice A and C are correct. In the functional paradigm, functions are pure (have no side effects) and always produce the same output

6 DATAFLOW PROGRAMMING WITH FUNCTIONS

for the same input. As a result, they behave similarly to a data processing component in the dataflow programming paradigm. Moreover, having a shared interface for input and output is the key for functions to connect with each other.

6.6.3 Quiz 3

Choice B is correct. The pipe operator `|>` allows us to pass an argument to a function from left to. Its type is `(|>) : 'a -> ('a -> 'b) -> 'b`. Consequentially, `2 |> square` is equivalent to `square 2`.

6.6.4 Quiz 4

Choice C is correct. The program checks if all integers in the input list are positive. Since `0` is not a positive number, the result is `false`.

6.6.5 Quiz 5

Choice B and C are correct. Streams allow us to model infinite sequences of data. Moreover, streams allow us to benefit from incremental computation since data is calculated on demand.

6 DATAFLOW PROGRAMMING WITH FUNCTIONS

6.6.6 Quiz 6

Choice C is correct. This expression implements a dataflow program that consists of the following processing steps:

- Select all elements from the lists that are greater than or equal to 3. In this case, the filtered list is [3; 4]
- Double the list elements to [6; 8]
- Fold right the list using the (+) function with the initial value 0. This is equivalent to summing up all list elements. The sum is 6 + 8 = 14.

6.6.7 Quiz 7

Choice B is correct. The OCaml keyword `lazy` delays the evaluation of an expression. That means, the evaluation of 1/0 is delayed and hence no `Division by zero` exception occurs.

6.6.8 Quiz 8

Choice A is correct. Here, `expr` is a delayed evaluation of 1/0. `Lazy.force` forces 1/0 to evaluate which causes a `Division by zero` exception.

7 Applying Functional Programming in Practice

7.1 Handle Collections in Data Processing Applications

There is an entrenched myth in the software industry that functional programming was invented by university researchers for "math stuff." Functional programming is widely considered less relevant for real-world software applications, such as food delivery, ride-hailing, and e-commerce. Yet, more and more software engineers discover that functional programming is an elegant paradigm to solve many data processing problems in enterprise applications.

This section particularly looks into how functional programming allows us to elegantly handle collections of data commonly found in mobile and web applications or backend services.

7.1.1 The map, filter, and fold functions are almost enough

Even though there are infinitely many problems to solve when processing data collections, most issues boil down to transforming, filtering, and accumulating data. Due to this, we combine `map`, `filter`, and `fold` to achieve most collection processing tasks.

To illustrate, let's say we work on an e-commerce application where we need to handle products. In OCaml, we could use the record type to represent a product. For the sake of simplicity, we only consider the product's name, type, and price.

7 APPLYING FUNCTIONAL PROGRAMMING IN PRACTICE

```
(* OCaml *)
type product_type = ELECTRONIC | BOOK |
    COSMETIC
type product = { name: string; product_type:
    product_type; price : float}
```

When we can store a collection of products in a list.

```
(* OCaml *)
let products = [{name = "iPad"; product_type =
    ELECTRONIC ; price = 800.0}; {name = "
    Pride and Prejudice"; product_type = BOOK;
    price = 10.0}; {name = "Mac Pro";
    product_type = ELECTRONIC; price =
    2000.0}; {name = "Smart TV"; product_type
    = ELECTRONIC; price = 500.0}]
```

Given such a collection of products, we typically want to do calculations on it. For example, we can calculate the total price of all electronic products. This kind of problem is ideal for `map`, `filter`, and `fold`. In particular, we can formulate a dataflow program where the product collection flows through three stages:

- Stage 1: Choose products that are electronic products with `filter`.
- Stage 2: Extract the price of each electronic product with `map`.
- Stage 3: Accumulate the total price with `fold`.

We can visualize this solution as the following dataflow diagram:

7 APPLYING FUNCTIONAL PROGRAMMING IN PRACTICE

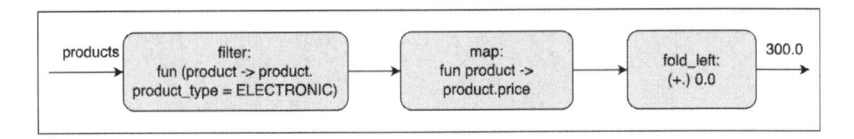

Figure 80: Calculate total price of electronic products

The following OCaml code implements that dataflow diagram:

```
1  (* OCaml *)
2  products |> List.filter (fun product ->
       product.product_type = ELECTRONIC) |> List
       .map (fun product -> product.price) |>
       List.fold_left (+.) 0.
3  (* Result: 3300. *)
```

As powerful as `map`, `filter`, and `fold` are, they're pretty generic. For practical purposes, it's often meaningful to define additional reusable, specialized functions for collections. This allows us to compose solutions for collection processing more conveniently. Often those specialized functions can be formulated using `map`, `filter`, and `fold`. In the remainder of this section, we'll discuss several such functions on collections.

7.1.2 Retrieve single elements

When working with collections, we often want to retrieve single elements from them. For instance, we might want to find the first product with a price less than a threshold. This problem is a particular case of finding the first element in a collection satisfying a predicate.

7 APPLYING FUNCTIONAL PROGRAMMING IN PRACTICE

One possible way to formulate such a function in OCaml is to use `List.filter` to filter out elements and `List.hd` to extract the first element of the resulting list.

```ocaml
(* OCaml *)
let find p l = List.filter p l |> List.hd
```

Note that if no element is found, the function throws an exception.

In fact, OCaml's `List` module already provides a `find` function that does precisely what we need. Let's use it to find the first product cheaper than 1000.

```ocaml
(* OCaml *)
List.find (fun product -> product.price <= 1000.0) products

(* Result: {name = "iPad"; product_type = ELECTRONIC; price = 800.} *)
```

We can view `find` as a dataflow component.

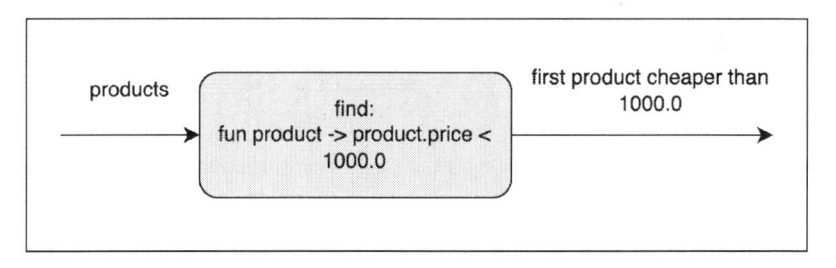

Figure 81: 'find' as a dataflow component

This `find` function only makes sense for an ordered collection. For an unordered collection, such as a set, we might change its semantics a bit to return some element that satisfies a given predicate.

We can also formulate a higher-order function called `contains` that checks whether any element in a list satisfies a given predicate.

```ocaml
(* OCaml *)
let contains p l = List.filter p l <> []

contains (fun product -> product.price <=
    1000.0) products
(* Result: true *)
```

7.1.3 Order collection elements

Sorting is another exceedingly important operation when processing ordered collections. OCaml's List provides a `sort` function that takes a compare function and a list as inputs and returns a sorted list.

For our e-commerce application, when the user chooses to display the products from low to high price, we can use `sort` to achieve that. We can use OCaml's built-in function, `Stdlib.compare`, to compare the prices of two products of type float.

```ocaml
(* OCaml *)
List.sort (fun product1 product2 -> Stdlib.
    compare product1.price product2.price)
    products

(* Result: [{name = "Pride and Prejudice";
    product_type = BOOK; price = 10.}; {name =
    "Smart TV"; product_type = ELECTRONIC;
    price = 500.}; {name = "iPad";
    product_type = ELECTRONIC; price = 800.};
```

7 APPLYING FUNCTIONAL PROGRAMMING IN PRACTICE

```
    {name = "Mac Pro"; product_type =
    ELECTRONIC; price = 2000.}] *)
```

Another useful operation is reversing a collection. We can use `List.fold_right` to formulate a `reverse` function in OCaml.

```
1  (* OCaml *)
2  reverse l = List.fold_right (fun x acc -> acc
       @ [x]) l []
3
4  reverse products
5  (* Result: [{name = "Smart TV"; product_type =
       ELECTRONIC; price = 500.}; {name = "Mac
       Pro"; product_type = ELECTRONIC; price =
       2000.}; {name = "Pride and Prejudice";
       product_type = BOOK; price = 10.}; {name =
       "iPad"; product_type = ELECTRONIC; price
       = 800. *)
```

7.1.4 Retrieve collection parts

We may want to retrieve only some parts of a collection when processing it. In instance, in our e-commerce application example, the user may want to see only the top two cheapest products. For this kind of use case, we can define a convenient operation called `take`, which takes the first n elements from a given collection.

In OCaml, we can implement `take` as a function on a list, as shown below:

```
1  (* OCaml *)
2  let rec take n l =
3    if n <= 0 then [] else match l with
4                          | [] -> []
```

The Art of Functional Programming

```
5            | hd :: tl -> hd ::
                     (take (n-1) tl)
```

The function accepts two arguments, an integer n and a list l. It returns a new list that contains the n first elements from l. If n is greater than the list length, the result has the same elements as l.

We can use this function to show the top two cheapest products, as shown below:

```
1  (* OCaml *)
2  List.sort (fun product1 product2 -> Stdlib.
       compare product1.price product2.price)
       products |> take 2
3  (* Result: [{name = "Pride and Prejudice";
       product_type = BOOK; price = 10.}; {name =
       "Smart TV"; product_type = ELECTRONIC;
       price = 500.}] *)
```

We can define a more general, higher-order function called take_while, which keeps taking elements from a collection that satisfies a predicate. It stops before the first element that does not match the predicate.

Below is how we can implement take_while in OCaml:

```
1  (* OCaml *)
2  let rec take_while p l =
3      match l with
4      | [] -> []
5      | hd :: tl -> if p hd then hd :: (
           take_while p tl) else []
```

When we use this function, we can only show products from the low-

7 APPLYING FUNCTIONAL PROGRAMMING IN PRACTICE

est to the highest price, as long as they are cheaper than 1000.0, as shown below:

```ocaml
(* OCaml *)
List.sort (fun product1 product2 -> Stdlib.
    compare product1.price product2.price)
    products |> take_while (fun product ->
    product.price < 1000.)

(* Result: [{name = "Pride and Prejudice";
    product_type = BOOK; price = 10.}; {name =
    "Smart TV"; product_type = ELECTRONIC;
    price = 500.}; {name = "iPad";
    product_type = ELECTRONIC; price = 800.}]
*)
```

7.1.5 Domain-specific language for collections

We have essentially defined a domain-specific language (DSL) for collections in this section. In particular, we use the list datatype to store collection elements. Next, we define various functions and higher-order functions that capture common patterns for operating over collections.

The following diagram graphically depicts how the collection DSL is defined on top of OCaml:

7 APPLYING FUNCTIONAL PROGRAMMING IN PRACTICE

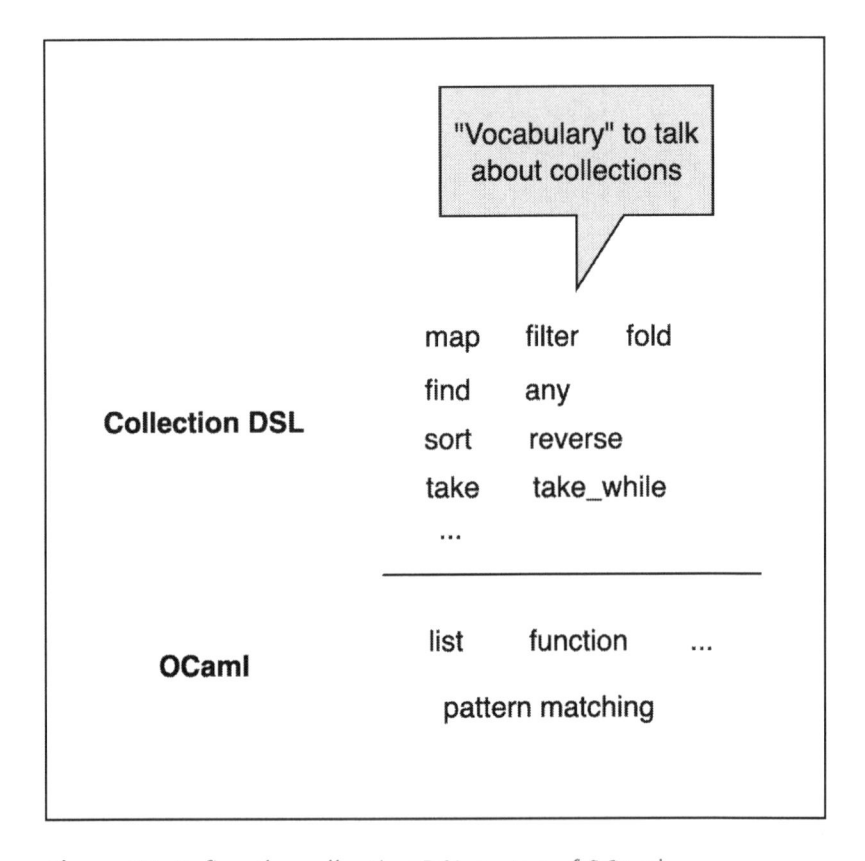

Figure 82: Define the collection DSL on top of OCaml

The DSL for collections allows us to think and program on a higher abstraction level because we can treat the entire collection of elements as a single unit. There is no need to name and work with collection elements individually. Furthermore, we can compose functions to leverage the elegance of the dataflow programming paradigm to solve collection processing problems. This is possible because the collection serves as a shared interface.

7   APPLYING FUNCTIONAL PROGRAMMING IN PRACTICE

We can use techniques from this section to handle collections of data when developing mobile or web applications in other programming languages, such as Swift, Kotlin, JavaScript, and Java. The functional style makes the code very readable while maximizing code reusability because the solutions are built by composing existing operations with each other.

7.2 Handle JSON

Functional programming is an excellent fit for processing hierarchical data structures, such as formal languages or data formats. In this lesson, we'll use OCaml to represent and manipulate JSON – a text-based data exchange format widely used to exchange data across the network, such as in web services. Handling JSON provides us with an excellent opportunity to apply many of the techniques we've learned, including algebraic datatypes, functions, and higher-order functions.

The following example shows a possible JSON representation describing the classic movie "The Godfather." For the sake of simplicity, we'll list only three actors in this example:

```
{
  "title": "Godfather",
  "genre": [
    "crime",
    "drama"
  ],
  "year": 1972,
  "actors": [
    {
```

7 APPLYING FUNCTIONAL PROGRAMMING IN PRACTICE

```
10        "actor": "Marlon Brando",
11        "character": "Vito Corleone",
12        "is_major_character": true
13      },
14      {
15        "actor": "Al Pacino",
16        "character": "Michael Corleone",
17        "is_major_character": true
18      },
19      {
20        "actor": "Lenny Montana",
21        "character": "Luca Brasi",
22        "is_major_character": false
23      }
24    ],
25    "is_on_netflix": true
26  }
```

A JSON structure like the one above may be used by a desktop application to store movie data. It might also come from a web service, like REST API, which provides movie information.

7.2.1 Represent JSON as an algebraic data type

To figure out how to represent the JSON structure in OCaml, we have to think about the different ways to define a valid JSON. The simplest valid JSON can be one of the following primitive values:

- A null value
- A string such as `"Hello"`
- An integer such as `123`
- A float value such as `12.34`
- A boolean value such as **true** or **false**

7 APPLYING FUNCTIONAL PROGRAMMING IN PRACTICE

There're two ways to build a more complex JSON, as shown below:

- A JSON array of values, such as `["crime", "drama"]`. Notice that the array elements can be any JSON. Furthermore, the elements might have different types, for example, `["Hello", 42, true]`.

- A JSON object, which begins with a left brace { and ends with a right brace }. Inside the braces is a collection of key-value pairs delimited by commas , where the key is a string and the value is any JSON. For example:

```
{
    "title": "Godfather",
    "genre": [
        "crime",
        "drama"
    ],
    "year": 1972
}
```

The JSON structure is hierarchical and characterized by various cases. As a result, it can be represented naturally by an algebraic data type, as shown below:

```
(* OCaml *)
type json = Null
          | String of string
          | Int of int
          | Float of float
          | Bool of bool
          | Array of json list
          | Object of (string * json) list
```

7 APPLYING FUNCTIONAL PROGRAMMING IN PRACTICE

Note that we use a list to represent a JSON array. Moreover, we represent a JSON object as a list of pairs of type (string * json), where the key is a string and the value is a JSON.

7.2.2 Pretty print JSON

After we declare an algebraic datatype to represent the JSON structure, the next step is to implement the pretty print functionality. In particular, we'll write a `json_to_string` function that converts a JSON object to a string.

For that, we go over each data constructor of the JSON type from the previous section and think about how to pretty print it. It's relatively straightforward in the case of primitive values.

- For `Null`, we print an empty string.
- For `String s`, we print s wrapped in quotation marks "s".
- For `Int i`, `Float f`, and `Bool b`, we convert the integer, float, or boolean value inside the constructor into a string. OCaml already provides a host of built-in functions to convert various types into strings, such as `string_of_int`, `string_of_float` and `string_of_bool`.

In the case of a JSON array, we pretty print each element and concatenate them with a comma. A similar idea applies to pretty print a JSON object.

The following OCaml code shows a possible implementation of `json_to_string`:

7   APPLYING FUNCTIONAL PROGRAMMING IN PRACTICE

```ocaml
(* OCaml *)
let rec json_to_string js =
  match js with
  | Null -> ""
  | String s -> "\"" ^ s ^ "\""
  | Int i -> string_of_int i
  | Float f -> string_of_float f
  | Bool b -> string_of_bool b
  | Array l -> let ss = List.map
      json_to_string l in "[" ^ (String.
      concat "," ss) ^ "]"
  | Object l -> let ss = (List.map (fun (key,
      value) -> "\"" ^ key ^ "\"" ^ ":" ^ (
      json_to_string value) ) l) in "{" ^ (
      String.concat "," ss) ^ "}"

let movie =
  Object
    [("title", String "Godfather");
     ("genre", Array [String "crime"; String "
        drama"]);
     ("year", Int 1972);
     ("actors",
        Array [Object [("actor", String "
           Marlon Brando");
                       ("character", String "
                          Vito Corleone");
                       ("is_major_character",
                          Bool true)];
               Object [("actor", String "Al
                  Pacino");
                       ("character", String "
                          Michael Corleone");
                       ("is_major_character",
                          Bool true)];
               Object [("actor", String "Lenny
                   Montana");
                       ("character", String "
```

7 APPLYING FUNCTIONAL PROGRAMMING IN PRACTICE

```
                              Luca Brasi");
26                          ("is_major_character",
                              Bool false)]]);
27                          ("is_on_netflix", Bool
                              true)]
28
29  json_to_string movie
30  (* Result: "{"title":"Godfather","genre":["
       crime","drama"],"year":1972,"actors":[{"
       actor":"Marlon Brando","character":"Vito
       Corleone","is_major_character":true},{"
       actor":"Al Pacino","character":"Michael
       Corleone","is_major_character":true},{"
       actor":"Lenny Montana","character":"Luca
       Brasi","is_major_character":false}],"
       is_on_netflix":true}" *)
```

The string representation of JSON returned by `json_to_string` does not take new lines and indentations into account. But we can reformat it with a JSON beautifier.

7.2.3 Extract fields from JSON

We defined an algebraic datatype to represent JSON and a function to pretty print it. Next, let's provide the ability to extract data from a JSON. For example, given a JSON representing a movie, we might want to extract `title` to figure out the movie's title. For that, let's write a `member: string -> json -> json` function that takes as arguments a field name and a JSON. This function returns the JSON associated with the field name. The only case where we can extract data via a field name is `Object`. In all other cases, we simply return `Null`.

7 APPLYING FUNCTIONAL PROGRAMMING IN PRACTICE

The following OCaml code shows a possible implementation of `member` and how it can be used to extract the `actors` field from the `movie` JSON:

```ocaml
(* OCaml *)
let member field json =
  match json with
  | Null -> Null
  | String _ -> Null
  | Float _ -> Null
  | Int _ -> Null
  | Bool _ -> Null
  | Array _ -> Null
  | Object records -> let record = List.find
      (fun record -> fst record = field)
      records in snd record

movie |> member "actors" |> json_to_string
(* Result: "[{"actor":"Marlon Brando","character":"Vito Corleone","is_major_character":true},{"actor":"Al Pacino","character":"Michael Corleone","is_major_character":true},{"actor":"Lenny Montana","character":"Luca Brasi","is_major_character":false}]" *)
```

In the code above, we use the pretty print function defined in the previous section to make the output more readable. We also use the pipe operator |> to chain one function to the next to make the data flow from left to right.

7 APPLYING FUNCTIONAL PROGRAMMING IN PRACTICE

7.2.4 Higher-order functions on JSON

Whenever we define an algebraic datatype to represent a hierarchical structure, it's good practice to think about meaningful high-order functions on that type. In this section, we'll define several higher-order functions that serve as general computation patterns on JSON.

Higher-order functions on a JSON array

We apply a function to its elements to transform a JSON array into a new one. For example, the following JSON array contains a list of actors who were in "The Godfather":

```
[
    {
        "actor": "Marlon Brando",
        "character": "Vito Corleone",
        "is_major_character": true
    },
    {
        "actor": "Al Pacino",
        "character": "Michael Corleone",
        "is_major_character": true
    },
    {
        "actor": "Lenny Montana",
        "character": "Luca Brasi",
        "is_major_character": false
    }
]
```

Below is how we can make it more compact:

```
[
```

7 APPLYING FUNCTIONAL PROGRAMMING IN PRACTICE

```
 2    {
 3      "actor": "Marlon Brando plays Vito
               Corleone as a major character"
 4    },
 5    {
 6      "actor": "Al Pacino plays Michael Corleone
               as a major character"
 7    },
 8    {
 9      "actor": "Lenny Montana plays Luca Brasi
               as a supporting character"
10    }
11 ]
```

For this kind of transformation, we can define a general higher-order function called `json_array_map`. This higher-order function applies a function to each element of a JSON array.

```
 1  (* OCaml *)
 2  let json_array_map f json =
 3    match json with
 4    | Array l -> Array (List.map f l)
 5    | _ -> failwith "Not a JSON array"
 6
 7  let to_string json = match json with
 8                      | String s -> s
 9                      | _ -> failwith "Not a
                              JSON string"
10  let to_bool json = match json with
11                      | Bool b -> b
12                      | _ -> failwith "Not a
                              JSON boolean"
13
14  let to_compact_actor obj =
15    let actor = (member "actor" obj |>
               to_string) and
16        character = (member "character" obj |>
```

The Art of Functional Programming   275

7 APPLYING FUNCTIONAL PROGRAMMING IN PRACTICE

```
17                to_string) and
           is_major = (member "is_major_character"
               obj |> to_bool)
18      in
19      let character_type = if is_major then "
           major character" else "supporting
           character"
20      in Object [("actor", String (actor ^ "
            plays " ^ character ^ " as a " ^
            character_type))]
21
22    movie |> member "actors"  |> json_array_map
          to_compact_actor |> json_to_string
23    (* Result: "[{"actor":"Marlon Brando plays
          Vito Corleone as a major character"},{"
          actor":"Al Pacino plays Michael Corleone
          as a major character"},{"actor":"Lenny
          Montana plays Luca Brasi as a supporting
          character"}]" *)
```

We can also formulate a higher-order function, json_array_filter, to filter out elements of a JSON array that satisfy a given predicate. We can use this function to select only the movie's main characters.

```
1  (* OCaml *)
2  let json_array_filter p json =
3    match json with
4    | Array l -> Array (List.filter p l)
5    | _ -> failwith "Not a JSON array"
6
7  movie |> member "actors" |> json_array_filter
        (fun obj -> member "is_major_character"
        obj |> to_bool) |> json_to_string
8  (* Result: "[{"actor":"Marlon Brando","
        character":"Vito Corleone","
```

7 APPLYING FUNCTIONAL PROGRAMMING IN PRACTICE

```
is_major_character":true},{"actor":"Al
Pacino","character":"Michael Corleone","
is_major_character":true}]" *)
```

Higher-order functions on a JSON object

A JSON object is a collection of key-value pairs. As a result, we can define a map function, `json_object_map`. This function maps each key-value pair to a new key-value pair. For instance, we can use this function to transform `actors` into a more compact form in `movie`. To achieve that, we provide `json_object_map` with a map function that replaces `actors` with a new JSON array, while mapping other fields to themselves.

```
1  (* OCaml *)
2  let json_object_map f json =
3    match json with
4    | Object records -> Object (List.map f records)
5    | _ -> failwith "Not a JSON object"
6
7
8  let to_compact_actor obj =
9    let actor = (member "actor" obj |> to_string) and
10       character = (member "character" obj |> to_string) and
11       is_major = (member "is_major_character" obj |> to_bool)
12   in
13   let character_type = if is_major then " major character" else "supporting character"
14   in Object [("actor", String (actor ^ " plays " ^ character ^ " as a " ^ character_type))]
```

The Art of Functional Programming 277

7 APPLYING FUNCTIONAL PROGRAMMING IN PRACTICE

```
15
16
17  json_object_map (fun (key, value) ->
18    let actors = if key = "actors" then
          json_array_map to_compact_actor value
          else value
19    in (key, actors)) movie |> json_to_string
20  (* Result: "{"title":"Godfather","genre":["
      crime","drama"],"year":1972,"actors":[{"
      actor":"Marlon Brando plays Vito Corleone
      as a major character"},{"actor":"Al Pacino
       plays Michael Corleone as a major
      character"},{"actor":"Lenny Montana plays
      Luca Brasi as a supporting character"}],"
      is_on_netflix":true}" *)
```

Finally, let's define a filter function for JSON object called `json_object_filter`. It takes a JSON object as an input and returns a new JSON object. The latter contains only the key-value pairs that satisfy a predicate. With this function, we can easily construct a JSON object with fields identical to the fields of `movie`, but exclude the `is_on_netflix` field.

```
1  (* OCaml *)
2  let json_object_filter p json =
3    match json with
4    | Object records -> Object (List.filter p
        records)
5    | _ -> failwith "Not a JSON object"
6
7  movie |> json_object_filter (fun (key, value)
      -> key <> "is_on_netflix") |>
      json_to_string
8  (* Result: "{"title":"Godfather","genre":["
      crime","drama"],"year":1972,"actors":[{"
      actor":"Marlon Brando","character":"Vito
```

7 APPLYING FUNCTIONAL PROGRAMMING IN PRACTICE

```
Corleone","is_major_character":true},{"
actor":"Al Pacino","character":"Michael
Corleone","is_major_character":true},{"
actor":"Lenny Montana","character":"Luca
Brasi","is_major_character":false}]}" *)
```

In this section, we define a DSL for JSON. This JSON DSL allows us to represent and manipulate JSON on a high level of abstraction. In general, a functional programming language equipped with algebraic datatypes makes it extremely easy and convenient to define DSLs. Keep this in mind when deciding whether to use the functional paradigm for the problem at hand or not.

8 Conclusion

8.1 Wrap Up

We covered quite a lot of materials in this book. But if you ask me, "what are the most vital ideas to take away from the book?" my answer would be: functional programming excels at abstraction and composition.

Let's first review abstraction. We've seen that functions are the primary means to form computations that work on any argument. A `square` function represents a method to compute the square of any number, not just the square of a particular one. Of course, there is nothing new about this because almost all programming languages, functional and imperative alike, rely on functions for this kind of abstraction. What's new is how functional programming treats functions as first-class citizens. This opens the door to defining higher-order functions that take other functions as input or return functions as output. Higher-order functions make it possible to define highly general computation methods, such as `accumulate`, `map`, `filter`, and `fold`. Abstraction is a crucial technique to programming, and functional programming is exceedingly good at it.

Composition, another essential technique, allows us to develop large software programs by composing smaller ones. Functional programming excels at composition due to several reasons. First, we saw that everything is an expression in the functional paradigm. For example, the `if` conditionals and functions are all expressions. Because of this, we can combine smaller expressions to form complex ones. Second, functions are pure in the functional paradigm – they always return the same output for the same input. Another defining feature of functional programming is that functions are defined on immutable data. This means a function does not modify the data state, but instead constructs new data for the input data. This implies that functions in functional programming are close to mathematical functions. This property allows us to compose functions to create new ones with ease. Furthermore, functions can be connected in the dataflow style by agreeing on a shared data structure for input or output. For instance, we can compose `map`, `filter`, and `fold` to construct dataflow programs because these functions rely on lists as a shared interface.

I hope the book has shown you how powerful and elegant functional programming is. I would even claim that functional programming is quite simple once we grasp its way of thinking. David Ogilvy, credited as "Father of Advertising", used to say that "big ideas are usually simple ideas". I can't agree more. Many big ideas in the functional programming paradigm – such as first-class functions, higher-order functions, pure functions, immutable data, currying, and partial application – might look scary at first but are inherently simple.

8.2 Where to Go from Here?

The best thing you can do is apply functional programming to your projects. Most mainstream programming languages – Kotlin, Java, JavaScript, Swift, Python, and Scala – readily support functional programming. There are many excellent books, tutorials, and blog posts about functional programming out there. Each will have its own merit, depending on what you want to dig deeper into. If you want to learn more about the functional way of thinking, I heartily recommend the following two masterpieces :

- *Structure and Interpretation of Computer Programs* (also known as SICP or the Wizard book) by MIT professors Harold Abelson and Gerald Jay Sussman, with Julie Sussman.
- *Thinking Functionally with Haskell* by Oxford professor Richard Bird.

The two books Real-world OCaml and Real world Haskell are excellent resources for those who want to learn more about OCaml and Haskell.

If you want to do functional programming in a particular language such as Scala, Java, Kotlin, Swift, Python, and more, you'll have no problem finding books, tutorials, or documentation to learn the particular syntax and idioms in that language. However, the fundamentals discussed in this book will remain valid regardless of the programming language.

Before ending the book, let's recall what we mentioned in the introduction. Mastering functional programming lies in the balancing act between striving to grasp the fundamental principles and applying them to real-world problems pragmatically. Thank you for sticking with this book on the art of functional programming. I hope you've learned a lot and enjoyed it as much as I did while writing this book.

Printed in Great Britain
by Amazon